Prosper Mérimée

Letters to an Unknown

Translated, with a Preface, by
Henri Pène du Bois

PREFACE

IF I knew the name of the Unknown, I would not tell it; but I do not know it. I am not deprived of the charm of mystery which these letters make one appreciate intensely. To them one may attach dreams and vague ideas. They are like life, for the best gift of life is the idea which it gives of something that is not in life.

They are real, and the best object of the real is to serve in the making of the ideal. But students may find in them notes on the manners of an epoch, documents on the state of mind of men and women who are famous, revelations of hearts that were complex and not easily defined; the sincere expression of an admirable individuality.

Prosper Mérimée was a familiar figure of the court of Napoleon III. He wrote for the Empress tales which he signed with his name as her jester. It was a frivolous and vain

court, as every fashionable, exclusive society is; but, like every fashionable, exclusive
society, it was a good school for a politician.
Woman was its sovereign; nothing was done
in it but through her and for her.

Well, woman is man's great educator.
She teaches him the charming virtues, po-
liteness, discretion, and the pride which
fears to be importunate.   She teaches to
some the art of pleasing; to all, the useful
art of not displeasing.   One may learn from
her that society is more delicately composed than the frequenters of primaries
think.

From her one may absorb the idea that
the dreams of sentiment and the shadows of
faith are invincible, and that it is not Reason
which governs the world.   It is not Reason
which governs the world, and I suppose that
is why Mérimée, who was a member of the
Senate, an eloquent speaker, and an impres-
sive tactician in debate, said that politics
bored him.

He was, like the Baron Dominique-Vivant
Denon, who was a familiar figure of the court
of Napoleon I. and a friend of Josephine,

incapable of comprehending Christian asceti-
cism. Like the Baron Dominique-Vivant
Denon, he was skeptical in matters of faith,
a former secretary of legation, a director of
the Department of Fine Arts, a member
of the Institut de France, an officer of the
Legion of Honor, a graceful writer, a mediocre painter, and a collector of art objects.

Like the Baron Dominique-Vivant Denon,
he lived among furniture carved by Buhl,
among fine paintings, scarce books, antique
bronzes, painted vases, enamels, medals
gathered in a pother of errant and sagely
inquisitive life. Unlike the Baron Dominique-Vivant Denon, who went through the
Terror smiling, tranquil, curious, favored by
the people after having been favored by the
king, Mérimée was unpopular.

Six months after his death, the rioters
among the Communists set fire to his apartment on the Rue de Lille, and nothing was
saved from the ruins of it, except the frag-
ments of a Turkish pipe and a deformed
antique bronze, which I saw in Paris in the
house of M. Edouard Grenier. Paintings,
books, vases, enamels, medals, manuscripts,

letters, were destroyed. That is why there
are no letters of the Unknown.

Mérimée was not liked by the people, nor
by Hugo, Banville, Gautier, Goncourt, and
George Sand, and he returned their dislike
with interest. He found on George Sand's
table one day, while he was waiting for her
in her drawing-room, a portrait of him in
prose, which she had written, and he read
aloud the first lines of it.

George Sand, half-dressed, rushed into the
drawing-room and tore the manuscript from
his hands. He said: " These lines are true,
perhaps, but they are not flattering. I confess I am sorry I was honest and did not steal
them. I would have burned them."

Goncourt made the following entry in his
diary, November 1, 1865: " Mérimée talks
slowly, as if he were distilling words, and
as he talks he makes glacial coldness fall
around him. His irony is dry, wicked, astonishing, and domineering." But the bad
effect of this impression is tempered in the
same diary by a preceding entry, as follows:
" Mérimée is a being fashioned solely by
fear of ridicule. He was scolded when a

child, and as he was going out of the room
he heard his parents laugh at his tears.   He
swore he would never be laughed at again;
that is the reason of his dryness."

His dryness was only apparent.   He was
extremely sensitive, and he exaggerated indifference to make of it an armor.   He has
written in " Colomba," in " Carmen," and
in the incomparable fantasy of " Lokis,"
masterpieces of style and imagination which
compel admiration for his art.   He has written in his " Letters to an Unknown " tender, loyal, deeply pathetic confessions of
a temperament which imposes profound
affection.

HENRI PÈNE DU BOIS.

Letters to an Unknown

I.

PARIS, *Thursday*.

I HAVE received your letter. Everything is mysterious in you, and the same causes make you act in a manner precisely opposed to other mortals. You go to the country, very well! It means that you shall have the time to write; for there the days are long, and having nothing to do leads one to writing letters. At the same time, the watchfulness and the anxiety of your dragon being less troubled by the regulated occupations of the city, you shall be subjected to more questions when letters come to you. Then, in a castle, the coming of a letter is an event.

Not at all! You cannot write, but you can receive a multitude of letters. I am beginning to understand your ways, and to be hardly surprised at anything. I pray you, spare me, and do not inflict too harsh a trial on the unfortunate disposition which I have taken, I do not know how, to think well of everything which comes from you.

I remember having been a little too frank in my last letter on the subject of my temperament. An old diplomat friend of mine, a very clever man, has told me often not to speak ill of myself. "Your friends will speak ill of you enough." I am beginning to fear that you might take too literally all the ill that I told of myself. Imagine that my great virtue is modesty; I carry it to excess, and I tremble lest it should harm me in your opinion. Some other time, when I feel better inspired, I will give you the exact list of all my qualities. It will be a long list. To-day, I am ill, and dare not throw myself into this geometrical progression.

Guess where I was Saturday night, what I was doing at midnight. I was on the platform of one of the towers of Notre Dame, drinking orange water and eating ices

in the company of four of my friends and
of an admirable moon; the whole presided
over by a big owl beating its wings around
us. Paris in the moonlight, at that hour,
is truly a very beautiful spectacle. It
resembles the cities of the Arabian Nights,
where the inhabitants were enchanted during their sleep. Our party was singular
enough: there were represented four nations,
each one having a different point of view.
The trouble was, that some of us felt
obliged, in presence of the moonlight and
the owl, to assume a poetic tone and tell
commonplaces. Little by little everybody
talked out of reason.

I do not know how and by what associa-
tion of ideas that semi-poetic evening makes
me think of another which was not at all
poetic. I went to a ball given by young
friends of mine, where were invited all the
ballet girls of the Opera. These women are
mostly stupid; but I have remarked how
far superior they were in moral delicacy to
the men of their class. There is only one
vice which separates them from other women: that is poverty. All these rhapsodies

will edify you oddly.   So I hasten to finish
this letter.   Adieu.   Do not begrudge me
the flattered picture which I have made of
myself.

II.

FRANKNESS and truth are rarely good
things in regard to women; they are almost
always bad things.   Now you consider me
as a Sardanapalus because I went to a ball
of the Opera's ballet girls.   You reproach me
for that evening as if it were a crime, and
you reproach me for praising these poor girls
as if it were a greater crime still.   I repeat
it, make them rich, and there will remain
to them only good qualities.   But the aris-
tocracy has raised insurmountable barriers
among the different classes of society, in
order that one should not see how like the
things that happen on this side of the fence
are to those which happen on the other
side.   I want to tell you a story of the
Opera which I learned in that perverse company.   In a house of the Rue Saint-Honoré
lived a poor woman who never went out of

a small room under the roof for which she paid a rent of three francs a month. She had a daughter twelve years old, well kept, very demure, and who talked to nobody. This little girl went out three times a week, in the afternoon, and returned alone at midnight. The neighbors learned that she was a chorus girl at the Opera. One day, she goes down the stairs to the janitor's room and asks for a lighted candle. She gets it. The janitor's wife, astonished at her not returning, goes up to the garret, finds the woman dead on her bed, and the little girl busy burning an enormous quantity of letters which she took out of a very big box. She says: " My mother died to-night, and she has asked me to burn all her letters without reading them." That child has never known her mother's real name; she is absolutely alone in the world, and has no other resource than to be a vulture, a monkey, or a devil in the Opera's performances.

Her mother's last advice to her was to be very good, and a chorus girl at the Opera. She is very good, very devout and cares not to tell her story. Please tell me if this little girl has not infinitely more merit in leading the life that she leads, than you have, you who enjoy the singular happiness of irreproachable surroundings and of a temperament so refined that it summarizes in my view an entire civilization. I must tell you the truth. I bear bad company only at rare intervals, and through an inexhaustible curiosity about all the varieties of the human species. I never dare to come near the bad company of men. Something in it is too repulsive, especially at home, for my friends in Spain were always bull-fighters and muleteers. I have eaten more than once at table with people that an Englishman would not look at, for fear of losing the respect which he has for his own eye. I have even drunk from the same bottle as a convict. It must be said that there was no other bottle and that one must drink when one is thirsty. Do not think that I have a predilection for the rabble. I like simply to see other manners, other faces, to hear another language. Ideas are always the same, and if one eliminate all that is conventional I believe that there are good manners in places other than the Faubourg Saint Germain drawing-rooms.

The water color which I was making for you is turning out so badly that it is probable I will not send it to you. Let not this prevent you from sending me the worsted work which you are making for me. Try to select a good messenger. As a general rule never take a woman for a confidante; sooner or later you will repent if you do. Learn also that there is nothing so usual as to do evil for the pleasure of doing evil. Get rid of your optimism and realize that we are in this world to fight against everybody. In this connection, I shall tell you that a learned friend of mine, who reads hieroglyphics, says, that on the Egyptian coffins one reads often these two words: " Life, war "; which proves that I have not invented the maxim which I have just given to you.

III.

PARIS.

YOUR reproaches please me greatly. In truth, I am predestined by the fairies. I

ask myself often what I am to you, and
what you are to me. To the first question, I cannot get a reply; for the second
question, I imagine that I love you as if
you were a fourteen-year-old niece of mine
under my care. As for your relative who
is so moral and who speaks so ill of me, he
makes me think of Thwackum, who says
always: " Can any virtue exist without
religion ? " Have you read " Tom Jones,"
a book as immoral as all mine put together ?
If you were prohibited from reading it, you
read it most certainly. What an odd sort
of education is the one which you receive in
England! What is its use ? People lose
breath sermonizing a young girl for a long
time, and the result is that this young girl
desires to know precisely the immoral being
whom people tried to make her detest.
What an admirable history is that of the
serpent! . . .

I am studying you with vivid curiosity.
I have theories about little things—about
gloves, about boots, about curls, and so
forth, and I attach a great deal of importance to all this, because I have discovered

that there is a relation between the temperament of a woman and the whim or logic
which made her select such and such a stuff.
Thus, for example, the world owes to me
the demonstration of the fact that a woman
who wears a blue gown is a coquette, and
affects sentiment.   The demonstration is
easy, but it is long.   .   .   .

I went sailing the other day.   There was
a great quantity of sail-boats on the river
carrying all sorts of people.   There was a
very big boat in which were several women
of questionable manners.   From this boat
came a man about forty years of age, playing
on the tambourine for his own amusement.
While I was admiring the musical organization of that animal, a woman about twenty-
three years old came near him, called him a
monster, said that she had followed him from
Paris, and that if he would not admit her in
his company she would make him repent.
All this happened on the shore at a distance
of about twenty steps from our boat.   The
man played on the tambourine while the woman spoke, and replied to her very coldly
that he did not want her in his boat, where-

upon, she runs to the boat farthest from the shore and throws herself into the river, which splashes up on us in beastly fashion. Although she had put out my cigar, indignation did not prevent me from taking her out of the water before she had drunk two glasses. The beautiful object of so much despair had not budged, and he murmured between his teeth: " Why take her out of the water, since she wished to drown herself ?" We put the woman in a tavern, and, as it was late, and the dinner hour was near, we abandoned her to the care of the tavern-keeper's wife.

Why is it that women love best the men who are most indifferent to them ? That is what I asked myself, while going down the Seine, what I am asking myself again, and what I pray you to tell me, if you know.

IV.

I received your letter in one of those moments of melancholy when one sees life through a black glass. As your epistle is not very amiable—excuse my frankness—it

has contributed somewhat to keep me in a
sullen mood.   I wanted to reply to you
Sunday, immediately and dryly.   Immediately, because you had indirectly made a
sort of reproach to me, and dryly because I
was furious against you.   I was disturbed at
the first word of my letter, and this disturb-
ance prevented me from writing to you.
Thank the good Lord for this, for the
weather is fine to-day; my humor has become so much softened that I do not wish to
write to you any more save in a style of
honey and sugar.   I shall not quarrel with
you, therefore, about twenty or thirty passages of your last letter, which shocked me
greatly, and which I am willing to forget.
I forgive you, and with the more pleasure
because, in truth, I believe I love you better
when you are pouting than when you are in
another mood.   One passage of your letter
made me laugh alone for ten minutes.   You
say " short and sweet."   You say that you
are engaged for life as you would say: " I
am engaged for the quadrille."   Very well.
Apparently, I have employed my time well
disputing with you on love, marriage, and

the rest; you are still at the point of believ-
ing or of saying that when one says " Love,"
one loves.   Have you promised in a contract
signed before a notary, or on a paper with
a vignette at the head ?   When I was a
schoolboy I received from a dressmaker a
note surmounted by two hearts in flames
united by an arrow.   My teacher began by
taking the letter, and ended by putting me
in prison.   Then the object of this budding
passion consoled herself with my cruel
teacher.   Nothing is so fatal as engagements
to those for whom they are made.   Do you
know that if your love were promised, I
would think it impossible for you not to love
me ?   How could you not love me, you
who have made no promises to me, since
the first law of nature is to hold in horror
whatever has the air of an obligation ?   And,
in fact, every obligation is naturally bothersome.   In fine, if I had less modesty, I
would consider that if you had promised
your love to somebody, you will give it
to me, because you have promised me
nothing.   You seem to me to be devout,
even superstitious.   I am thinking at this

moment of a pretty little Granada girl who,
on mounting her mule to go through a
mountain pass, kissed her thumb and struck
her chest five or six times, persuaded after
this that robbers would not come, provided
the stranger did not swear too much. The
stranger was I, and his wicked manner of
talking was necessary in the bad spots of
the road in order to make the horses walk.
Read " Tristram Shandy."

V.

September 25th.

YOUR letter found me ill and sad, busy
with the most troublesome business, and I
have not the time to take care of myself.
I have decided not to quit Paris in October,
in the hope that you will come then. You
shall see me or not at your choice. The
fault will be yours. You speak of particular reasons which prevent you from trying to meet me. I do not ask what your
motives are. Only I pray you to tell me
really and truly if you have any. Are you

not preoccupied rather by some childish no-
tion ? Perhaps somebody read a sermon to
you about me. You should not be afraid of
me. Your natural prudence counts for
much, doubtless, in your disinclination to see
me. Be reassured, I shall not fall in love
with you. A few years ago, it might have
happened; now I am too old and I have
been too unfortunate. I came near falling
in love when I went to Spain. It is one of
the beautiful acts of my life. The woman
who was the cause of my voyage never knew
it. If I had remained, I would have done,
perhaps, something very foolish : I would
have offered to a woman worthy of all the
happiness that one may enjoy on earth, in
exchange for the loss of all the things that
were dear to her, a tenderness which I felt
was inferior to the sacrifice which she would
have made, perhaps. You recall my moral :
" Love excuses everything, but one must be
sure that it is love." Be persuaded that
this precept is more rigorous than those of
your Methodist friends. Conclusion : I shall
be charmed to see you. Perhaps you will
make the acquisition of a real friend, and I

will, perhaps, find in you a woman with
whom I shall not be in love and in whom I
may have confidence.   We shall probably
gain by better acquaintance.   Still, do what
your elevated prudence advises.

VI.

Do you know that you are sometimes
very amiable ?   I do not say this to send
you a reproach under a cold compliment;
but I should like to receive from you often
letters like your last one.   Unfortunately,
you are not always in moods as charitable.
I did not answer sooner because your letter
was given to me only last night at my return
from a small excursion.   I spent four days
in absolute solitude, without seeing a man,
much less a woman, for I do not call men
or women certain bipeds who are trained
to bring something to eat and to drink when
they receive the order to do so.   I made,
during this retreat, the saddest reflections
on myself, on my future, on my friends.
If I had had the wit to wait for your letter
it would have given quite another turn to

my ideas.   The remembrance of your splendid black eyes is perhaps an element of my
admiration for you.   Still, I am almost in-
sensible to beauty.   I say to myself that
" It spoils nothing; " but I assure you that
when I heard a man who is very hard to
please say that you were very pretty, I
could not prevent myself from feeling sad.
This is the reason: I am horribly jealous
of my friends, and it pains me to think that
your beauty exposes you to the cares and to
the attentions of a lot of men who cannot
appreciate you and who see in you only
what preoccupies me the least.   In truth, I
am in a frightful humor when I think of the
ceremony which you are to attend.   Nothing
makes me sadder than a marriage.   The
Turks, who bargain for a woman while they
examine them like fat sheep, are worth more
than we who have placed over this vile bargain a varnish of hypocrisy which is, alas,
quite transparent.   I have asked myself
often what I might say to a woman on the
first day of my wedding, and I have thought
of nothing possible, unless it be a compliment on her nightcap.   The devil, happily,

will be very clever if he should drag me
into such a festival. The part of a woman
is much more easy than that of a man. On
such a day as this she imitates Racine's
Iphigenie.

You shall never fall in love with me, do
not fear. The consoling predictions which
you make to me cannot be realized. The
chances of death for me have increased this
year. Be reassured about your letters. All
that shall be found in my room shall be
burned after my death; but to tease you
I will bequeath to you in my will a manuscript sequel to the " Guzla " which made
you laugh so much. You are an angel and
a demon, but more a demon than an angel.
You call me tempter. Dare to say that this
word does not fit you better than me.
Have not you thrown a bait to me, poor
little fish; then, now that you have me at
the end of your hook, you make me dance
between the sky and the water as long as you
please? When you are tired of the game,
you will cut the thread; then the hook will
be in my mouth, and I will not be able to
find the fisherman. Adieu, I promise not to

2

fall in love with you ever.   I do not want
to be in love, but I should like to have a
feminine friend.   Pity me, for I am very
sad and have a thousand reasons to be sad.

VII.

LADY M—— told me last night that you
were to be married.   This being so, burn
my letters; I burn yours, and good-by.   I
have already told you what my principles
were.   They do not permit me to remain in
friendly relations with a woman whom I
knew as a maid, with a widow whom I knew
when she was a married woman.   I have ob-
served that when the civil status of a woman
changed, her friendly relations with me
changed also, and always for the worse.   In
brief, right or wrong, I cannot endure that
my women friends should marry.   Therefore, if you marry, let us forget each other.
I pray you not to have recourse to one of
your ordinary means of escape, but to reply
frankly.

Your marriage was one of the fatalities

which were to fall upon me.   The other
night, as I could not sleep, I reviewed in my
mind all the miseries which have troubled
me for a fortnight, and found only one compensation for them, which was your amiable
letter.   Now I wish I could stab the sun, as
the Andalusians say.   I had a superb stone,
well cut, brilliant, scintillating, admirable.
I believed it was a diamond which I should
not exchange for that of the Grand Mogul.
Not at all.   It is a false stone.   A chemist
friend of mine has just made the analysis of
it.   Imagine my disappointment.   I have
spent a great deal of time thinking of this
pretended diamond and of my good fortune
in finding it.   Now I must spend as much
time, if not more, in persuading myself that
it was only a false stone.

This is only an apologue.   I took dinner
day before yesterday with the false diamond, and made a sad face.   When I am
angry I handle well enough the rhetorical
figure called irony, and I praised the good
qualities of the diamond in the heaviest
style that I knew, and with glacial coolness.
I do not know why I tell you all this, since

we are to forget each other soon. Meanwhile, I love you still and recommend myself to your prayers.

VIII.

MY dear feminine friend, we are becoming very tender. You say to me, "Amigo de mi alma," which is very pretty in a feminine mouth. You give me no news of your health. You had said in a previous letter that my feminine friend was ill, and you should have known that I was anxious. Be more exact in the future. You complain of my reticence and you are mystery incarnate. What more do you want on the diamond story if not the name ? Details, perhaps; but they would be annoying to write, and they may amuse you some day when we shall have nothing to say to each other, seated face to face in armchairs near the fire. Listen to the dream which I had two nights ago and interpret it if you be sincere. Methought that we were in Valencia, in a beautiful garden, with a multitude of oranges and pomegranates. You were seated on a bench near

a hedge.   Opposite was a wall some six feet
in height, which separated the garden from
another garden which was much lower.
We were talking in Valencian, it seemed to
me.   *Nota bene :* I hardly understand Valencian.   What a queer tongue one speaks in a
dream, when one speaks a language which
one does not know!   I went up a stone
and looked into the lower garden.   There
was a bench near the wall, and on that bench
a sort of Valencian gardener and my diamond
listening to the gardener, who was playing
the guitar.   The sight put me in bad humor
instantly, but I gave no sign of this at first.
The diamond saw me with astonishment,
but did not budge nor seem disconcerted.
After a time I came down from the stone
and said to you in the most natural way,
and without referring to the diamond, that
it would be a good joke to push a big stone
over the wall.   That stone was very heavy.
You were very glad to help me, and without asking any questions—which is not natural to you.   By dint of pushing, we succeeded in placing the stone on the top of
the wall, and were preparing to push it over

when the wall itself yielded, crumbled, and we fell with the stone and the wall. I do not know the rest, for I woke up. So that you may understand the scene better, I send you a drawing of it. I could not see the gardener's face, and this enrages me.

You are very amiable. I have said it to you often for some time. You are very amiable to have replied to the question which I asked you recently. I need not tell you that your reply pleased me. You said, involuntarily, perhaps, several things which pleased me, and especially that the husband of a woman who resembled you would inspire you with real compassion. I believe you, and add that there would be nobody in the world more unfortunate, unless it were a man who loved you. You must be cold and sarcastic in your bad moods, with a pride that prevents you from saying: " I am wrong." Add to this your energy which must make you disdain tears and complaints.

Come to Paris soon, dear Mariquita, and make of me a lover. I will not be lonesome then, and, in compensation for this, I will make you very miserable with my moods.

Your writing has become careless and your letters are very short.   I am convinced that you have no love for anybody and will never have any.   However, you understand well enough the theory of love.   Good-by; I make all the possible wishes for your health, for your happiness, in order that you should not get married, in order that you should come to Paris; in order, in fine, that we should become friends.

IX.

WHAT is your trouble ?   Are you sick at heart ?   There are, in your last note, some mysterious phrases, like all your phrases, which seem to say this.   Between us, I do not think that you have had the enjoyment of that viscera called heart.   You have troubles of the mind, pleasures of the mind; but the viscera named heart is developed at twenty-five years of age only, in the forty-sixth degree of latitude.   You will knit your beautiful and black eyebrows and say: " The impudent man doubts that I have a heart," for that is the great preten-

sion nowadays.   Since so many novels and
poems of passion, so-called, have been written, all women pretend to have a heart.
Wait a little.   When you shall have a heart
for good, you shall tell me about it.   You
shall regret the good old days when you
were living only by the mind, and you shall
see that the evils which make you suffer
now are only pin-pricks in comparison with
the stabs which shall rain on you when the
days of passion come.

X.

You must know that the sea makes me
very sick, and is agreeable to me only when
I see it from the shore.   The first time that
I went to England I was so sick that it took
me fifteen days to regain my ordinary color,
which is that of the pale horse in the Apoc·
alypse.   Forgive me for speaking always of
the diamond.   What must be the sentiment of a man who is not an expert in
gems, to whom jewellers have said, " This
stone is false," and who sees it shine admirably nevertheless; who says to himself at

times: " If the jewellers do not know diamonds! If they deceive themselves, or wish
to deceive me!" I look at my diamond
from time to time, and, whenever I look at
it, I find it a real diamond. It is a pity that
I cannot make a conclusive chemical experiment with it. What think you ? If I saw
you, I would explain to you what is obscure
in this matter, and you would give me
some good advice, or, better still, you would
make me forget my diamond, real or false,
for there is no diamond which may stand
comparison with two beautiful black eyes.
Good-by; you do not deserve a long letter.
You send me only a few lines of careless
writing, and when you write three lines, two
of them make me angry.

XI.

YOU are charming, dear Mariquita, too
charming, even. I possess at once your portrait and your confidence, double happiness.
You were in a mood of kindness that day,
for your letter was long and amiable; but it
has one defect, it settles nothing. Shall I

see you or shall I not ?   That is the question.   I know how to solve it, but you do
not want to decide.   You are, as you will
be always, hesitating between your temperament and your convent habits.   Why do
you not wish me to see you on the promenade, for example, or at the British Museum ?

XII.

London, *December* 10th.

WHY do you not wish to see me ?   Nobody near you knows me, and my visit
would seem natural.   Your principal motive
seems to be the fear to do something improper, as they say here.   I do not take
seriously what you say of the fear which
you have of losing your illusions about me
when you know me better.   If this were
your real motive, you would be the first woman, the first human being whom such a
consideration prevented from satisfying her
desire or her curiosity.   Let us come to the
impropriety.   Is the thing improper in itself ?   No, for there is nothing simpler.

You know in advance that I will not eat you. The thing is improper, if it is improper, only with respect to the world. Observe that this word " world " makes us miserable from the day when we put on a dress that is uncomfortable, until the day of our death.

In sending me your portrait it seems to me that you gave proof of esteeming me highly enough to believe in my discretion. Why should you believe in it no longer ? The discretion of a man, and mine in particular, is the greater the more is demanded of him. Being sure of my discretion, you may see me. I will add, with my hand on my heart, that I see not the least impropriety in this. I will say more. If this correspondence is to be continued without our meeting ever, it becomes the most absurd thing in the world. I leave this to your reflections.

If I had more fatuity, I would rejoice at what you say of my diamond. But we can never fall in love with each other. Our acquaintance did not begin in a manner to lead us to that point. It is too romantic. As for the diamond, my travelling companion, while smoking his cigar, spoke of it without knowing my interest in it, and said some very sad things.   He does not seem to doubt that it is false.   I offer you a good friendship which I hope will be useful to us some day.   Good-by.

XIII.

PARIS, *February*, 1842.

SINCE you do not disdain my gifts, here are preserves of roses, jessamine, and bergamot.   I had promised you sandals and you refuse them with so much persistence that I ought to send them to you.   But since my return I have been robbed.   No more sandals.   I cannot find them.   Will you take this in exchange ?   Perhaps this Turkish mirror will please you better; for it seems to me that you are still more coquettish than you were in the year of grace, 1840.   It was in the month of December, and you wore striped silk stockings.   That is all I can remember.

I give nothing for nothing.   Before going

to Naples, you shall have the kindness to
take my orders, and to bring to me what I
shall ask for.   I will give you a letter to the
director of the Pompeii diggings, if such
things interest you.   You make of your
precious self so brilliant a portrait that I see
the time when we shall meet again adjourned
to the Greek kalends.   Meanwhile, preserve
the radiant physiognomy which I admired.

XIV.

PARIS, *March*, 1842.

YOU are rich; so much the better.   I
send you my compliments.   Rich, that is
free.   Your friend who had such a good idea
must have been an Auld Robin Gray; he
must have been in love with you; you will
not admit it, because you like mystery.   I
forgive you; we write to each other too seldom to quarrel.   Why should you not go to
Rome and to Naples for pictures and sunlight ?   You are worthy to comprehend
Italy, and you would return richer by several ideas and several sensations.   I do not

advise you to go to Greece. Your skin is not hard enough to resist all the ugly beasts that eat people there. Talking of Greece, since you preserve so well what is given to you, here is a blade of grass. I plucked it from the Anthela hill at Thermopylæ, in the place where the three hundred died.

Do you wish something more substantial from the Orient? I have given, unfortunately, all the beautiful things that I brought back. I would give you sandals, but you would wear them for others. No, thank you. If you wish preserves of roses and jessamine I have some, but accept them in haste or I shall eat them all. We write to each other so rarely that we have many things to say to each other. This is my history:

I saw my dear Spain again in the fall of 1840. I spent two months in Madrid, where I saw a funny revolution, beautiful bull fights, and the triumphant entry of Espartero. I lived in the house of an intimate friend who is a devoted sister to me. I went to Madrid in the morning and returned to dinner in the country with six women,

the eldest of whom was thirty-six years old.
Because of the revolution, I was the only
man who could go and come freely, so that
those six unfortunates had no other escort.
They spoiled me prodigiously. I was in love
with none, and perhaps I was wrong. At my
return to Paris I gave to myself the innocent
pleasure of printing a book without publish-
ing it. There were only one hundred and
fifty copies, which I gave to people who
pleased me. I would offer this scarcity to
you if you were worthy of it; but it is a
historical and pedantic work, so studded
with Greek and Latin that you could not
even bite it.

Last summer I got a little money. I got
three months' vacation and spent five running from Malta to Athens, and from Ephe-
sus to Constantinople. In these five months
I was not out of sorts for five minutes. At
Constantinople I saw the Sultan in patent
leather boots and black frock coat. There a
beautiful woman, on whose sandal I stepped
by accident, struck me with her fist, and
called me a "*giaour*." I had no other relation with the Turkish beauties. I saw at

Athens and in Asia the most beautiful monuments in the world, and the most beautiful
landscapes possible.

The drawback consisted in fleas and in
bugs as big as larks; so I never slept.   In
the midst of all this I have become old.
Represent your friend to yourself all gray.
And you, are you changed ?   I am waiting
with impatience for you to be less pretty in
order to see you.   In two or three years,
when you write to me tell me what you are
doing and when we are to meet.   Your
" respectful souvenir " made me laugh, and
also your pretension to dispute my heart
with Ionic and Corinthian columns.   In the
first place, I like only Doric columns, and
there are no columns, not excepting those
of the Parthenon, which are worth to me
the reminiscence of an old friendship.   Good-
by; go to Italy and be happy.

XV.

PARIS, *March*, 1842.

I HAVE just received your letter, which
has put me in bad humor.   So, it was your

satanical conceit which prevented you from
seeing me. I have not the right to make reproaches to you, for I saw you the other day,
I think, and a similar sentiment restrained
me at the moment when I was about to
talk to you. You say that you are better
than you were two years ago. You seem to
me to be more beautiful; but you seem to
have acquired selfishness and hypocrisy.
These may be useful; only, they are not
worth pluming one's self on. As for me, I
am worth, I think, neither more nor less than
formerly. I am not more a hypocrite than
I was. I am, perhaps, wrong. It is certain
that I am not loved more. Since this purse
was not embroidered by your white hands,
what do you wish me to do with it? You
ought to give me some work of yours; my
mirror and my preserves deserve one. At
least, you might have told me if you received them. When you go to Italy and
pass through Paris, it is probable you will
not see me there. Where shall I be? The
devil only knows. It may be that I will go
to Saragossa to see this woman about whom
you write that you are worth as much as

3

she. For a sister, I shall have no other.
Good-by; I am sorry that I did not see you.
Write to me from time to time. It will
give me always great pleasure to hear from
you, even if you continue the beautiful system of hypocrisy which you have begun so
triumphantly.

XVI.

PARIS, *May* 14, 1842.

YOU are much more beautiful physically,
but not morally. You have a beautiful complexion, and admirable hair, which I looked
at more than your bonnet, which is probably
worth the trouble of a look, since you are
irritated because of my lack of apprecia-
tion. But I never could distinguish laces
from calico. You have still the waist of a
sylph, and, although I am quite *blasé* about
black eyes, I never saw any as large in Constantinople or in Smyrna.

Now comes the reverse of the medal.
You have remained a child in many things,
and you have become a hypocrite in the
bargain. You do not know how to conceal

your first movements; but think you can repair them with a multitude of means. Your magnanimous idea to be harsh for yourself will lead you far, assuredly, and in a few years from now you will find yourself as happy as a Trappist who, after torturing himself, suddenly discovered that there was no Paradise.

I think I shall not go to Saragossa. I may go to Florence; but it is certain that I shall spend two months in the south of France looking at churches and Roman ruins. Perhaps we shall meet near a temple or a circus. I advise you to go directly to Naples. You might, however, if you stayed five or six hours at Leghorn, use your time better by going to Pisa to see the Campo-Santo. You promised me something in exchange for my Turkish mirror. I rely piously on your memory. Be happy, but retain this maxim, " If you do foolish things, do only those that please you."

XVII.

PARIS, *June 22*, 1842.

I HAVE received your purse; it exhaled a very aristocratic perfume and is very pretty. If you embroidered it yourself it does you honor. But I have recognized in it your recently acquired taste for material things: in the first place, it is a purse; in the second, you valued it a hundred francs at the stage coach. It would have been more poetical to declare that it was worth one or two stars; I prize it as highly. I will put medals in it. I would have cared for it more if you had deigned to put in it two or three lines from your white hand.

I do not want your pheasants; you offer them to me in an ugly fashion, and, moreover, you say disagreeable things to me about my Turkish preserves. It is you who have the palate of a *giaour* if you do not know how to appreciate what the Peris eat. The hypocrisy which you practise well enough will turn against you some day. It will become real. As for coquetry, which is the inseparable companion of the ugly vice that you praise, you have had it always. It became you well when you tempered it with frankness, heart, and imagination. Now . . . You have beautiful black hair and a beautiful blue cashmere shawl, and you are amiable when you wish. Say that I do not spoil you!

There was once a dervish who seemed to a baker to be a saint. The baker promised to give him white bread as long as he lived. The dervish was enchanted. After a period the baker said to him: " We have agreed on brown bread, haven't we? I have excellent brown bread, it is my specialty." The dervish replied: " I have more brown bread than I can eat; but . . ." I must tell you that I am spending my nights re-reading my works, which are being reprinted. I find them very immoral, and sometimes stupid. I must diminish the immorality and the stupidity without giving myself too much trouble. I say good-by to you, and kiss your hands humbly.

XVIII.

CHÂLON-SUR-SAÔNE, *June* 30, 1842.

YOU guessed correctly the end of the story: the dervish was mystified by the baker, but he did not like brown bread.

I saw in Saint Vincent church a very pretty young woman who was making stations of the cross. Is this not the right description for the prayers that are said before paintings representing the principal scenes of the passion ? Her mother was near her watching her very attentively. While taking notes on old Byzantine columns, I asked myself what this young girl could have done to deserve such a penance. The case must have been very grave. Have you become very pious, in accordance with the present fashion ? You must be pious for the same reason that you wear a blue cashmere shawl. I should be sorry if it were so; our devoutness in France displeases me; it is a sort of mediocre philosophy, which comes from the mind and not from the heart. When you shall have seen the devoutness of the people

of Italy, I hope that you will say, as I do,
that it is the only real devoutness.   .   .   .

XIX.

AVIGNON, *July* 20, 1842.

SINCE you take this view of it, I capitu-
late.   Give me brown bread, it is better
than nothing at all.   Only, permit me to
say that it is brown bread.   You see that I
am humble and submissive.   I shall reply to
your letter article by article.   The figure of
rhetoric which you think you have invented
has been known for a long time.   One
might give it a new name with the aid of
Greek.   In French it is simply a lie.   Use
it with me as little as you can.   Do not
abuse it with others.   Keep it only for great
occasions.   Do not try to find the world silly
and ridiculous.   You ought to try to represent it to yourself as it is not.   It is better
to have illusions than not to have any.

Your story is well known: " There was
once an idol   .   .   ." read Daniel; but he
was mistaken, the head was not of gold; it

was of clay, like the feet. But the idolater had a lamp in his hand and the reflection of this lamp gilded the idol's head. If I were the idol I would say: " Is it my fault that you have put out your lamp ?" It seems to me that I am becoming very Oriental.

I see with grief that your coquetry goes on increasing. I am well informed about your devoutness. I thank you for your prayers, if they are not a figure of rhetoric. I am very sorry that you are reading Homer through Pope. Everything in Homer is remarkable. The epithets which seem so strange when translated in French are admirably precise. I remember that he calls the sea purple, and I had never understood that word. Last year I was in a little boat on the Gulf of Lepanto. The sun was setting. As soon as it vanished, the sea took for ten minutes a magnificent dark violet tint. This requires the air, the sea, and the sun of Greece. I hope that you shall never become an artist enough to have pleasure in recognizing that Homer was a great painter. Good-by.

XX.

PARIS, *August* 27, 1842.

I WILL tell you how they call in Greek persons who have, like you, hair of which they are justly proud. The word is " efplokamos." " Ef," well, " plokamos," curl of hair. The two words reunited form an adjective. Homer said somewhere: " Nimfi efplokamouca Calypso." This means, " Calypso, nymph with well-curled hair." Isn't it pretty ? O, for the love of Greek, and so forth. . . .

I was packing my luggage at Avignon, when two venerable figures entered and announced themselves as members of the municipal council. I thought they were going to talk of some church, but they said pompously they had come to recommend to my loyalty and to my virtue a lady who was to travel in my company. I replied to them in very bad humor that I should be very loyal and very virtuous, but that it did not please me to travel with a woman, since I should not be able to smoke on the road.

The stage-coach arrived, and I found in it a
woman tall and pretty, simply and coquettishly dressed, who said that she was sick,
and despaired of reaching Paris alive.   I
was as polite and amiable as I could be.
My companion was a Bonapartist, was very
enthusiastic, believed in the immortality of
the soul, not much in the catechism, and
was an optimist.   I felt that she was in a
measure afraid of me.   At Moulins the
coach took two dull travellers, and at Paris
my mysterious lady precipitated herself into
the arms of a very homely man who must
have been her father.   I took off my cap to
him, and was getting into a carriage, when
my unknown came and said to me: " I am
moved, sir, by your kindness to me.   I cannot tell you enough how grateful I am.   I
will never forget the happiness which I have
had in travelling with a man so illustrious."
I am quoting the text.   But the word
" illustrious" explained the municipal council and the lady's fright.   It is evident that
they had seen my name on the post-office
book, and that the lady, who had read my
books, expected to be swallowed alive.

What gave you the idea to make my acquaintance ?

I shall be in Paris all the autumn, I think.
I shall work a great deal on a moral book,
as amusing as the social war which you are
to carry to Naples.   Good-by.   Alas!   I
have lost my most beautiful antique gem, a
magnificent Juno, while doing a good act—
that is, carrying a drunkard who had broken
his thigh; and this stone was Etruscan, and
the figure held a scythe, and there is no
other monument where Juno is so represented.   Pity me.

XXI.

YOUR Greek writing is charming, and
much more legible than your French.   But
who is your Greek teacher ?   You cannot
make me believe that you have learned to
write cursive letters from a printed book.

Your letter is very amiable.   I say this
because I know that compliments are agreeable to you, and also because it is true.
However, as I will never know how to cure
myself of the unfortunate fault of saying

what I think to people who are not everybody
to me, you must know that I see you making
rapid progress in satanism.   You are becoming ironical, sarcastic, and even diabolical.
All these words are taken from the Greek,
and your teacher will tell you what I mean
by diabolical; that is, calumniator.   You
mock my most beautiful qualities, and when
you praise me, you do it with reticences and
precautions which take from the praise all
its merit.   It is true that I have frequented
bad company, but I did it through curiosity,
and I was always in it as in a strange country.   As for good company, I have found it
often mortally boresome.   There are two
places wherein I am comfortable enough:
one among people without pretentiousness
whom I have known for a long time; two,
in a Spanish venta, with muleteers and
peasants of Andalusia.

XXII.

PARIS, *October* 24, 1842.

THE trouble with the Greeks is that their
ideas of decency and even of morality were

very different from ours. There are many
things in their literature which might shock
you, even disgust you, if you understood
them. After Homer you can read the tragedy writers, who will amuse you, and whom
you will like because you have a taste for
the beautiful, a sentiment which the Greeks
possessed in the highest degree, and which
a happy few have inherited from them. If
you have the courage to read history, Herodotus and Xenophon will charm you. Begin with the Anabasis. Then you will read
Herodotus, and, at last, Thucydides. I
would recommend also Lucian, who is the
wittiest Greek, but he is very wicked, and I
dare not. As for the pronunciation, I will
send you a page which I have prepared for
you. It will teach you the pronunciation of
the modern Greeks. That of the schools is
easier, but it is absurd.

XXIII.

Thursday, October, 1842.

WOULD you like to hear an Italian opera
with me to-day ? I have a box Thursdays,

with my cousin and his wife. They are travelling, and the box is wholly mine; you should have with you your brother or one of your relatives who does not know me. You would please me greatly by coming.

XXIV.

Friday morning, October, 1842.

I THANK you for having come yesterday. I hope your brother saw nothing extraordinary in our meeting. I have an Etruscan seal for you; I cannot endure the one that you are using.

XXV.

Tuesday night, October, 1842.

I DO not know where you have learned that I have friends in the four corners of the world. You know very well that I have only one woman friend in Madrid. Believe in my gratitude for your magnanimity toward me at the opera the other night. I appreciate as I should the condescendence with which you showed your face to me for two hours, and I must say that I admired it a great deal.   As for your assertion that you have never refused me anything, this lie will procure for you several million years of purgatory.   I see that you desire my Etruscan gem, and, as I am more magnanimous than you, I will not say, like Leonidas, "Come and take it!"   But how shall I send it to you ?

XXVI.

PARIS, *Tuesday night.*

YOU say, with a great deal of amiability, that you do not wish to see me for fear of boring me.   Unless I am mistaken, we have seen each other six or seven times in six years, and if we add the minutes, we may find that we have spent three or four hours together, half of the time saying nothing. As I have not the means to overcome your resolutions, this one will end as you will, but I think it silly not to see me.   I beg your pardon for this word, which is neither polite nor friendly, but, unfortunately, true. I ask of you nothing in exchange for my

antique seal, because you have refused everything that I have asked for.

XXVII.

PARIS, *Saturday, November,* 1842.

YOU ought to see me, if only to get out
of the atmosphere of flattery in which you
are living.   We ought to go together some
day to the museum to see Italian paintings.
It would be a great advantage to you to
have me for a cicerone.

XXVIII.

PARIS, *November,* 1842.

I WOULD like to know what you are doing.
When I see you so learned in Greek and in
German, I conclude that you are very lonesome, and spend your life with books and
some learned professors to explain them to
you.

XXIX.

PARIS, *December* 2, 1842.

THERE is a graceful tale in an old Spanish
novel.   A barber had a shop at the angle of

two streets, and the shop had two doors. Through one of these doors he went out and stabbed a passer-by, returned to his shop, went out through the other door, and bandaged his victim's wound. I bear no ill-will to your blue cashmere shawl, and your cakes. I hold coquetry and greediness in esteem, but only when they are confessed frankly. And you, who aspire to be something more than a woman in fashionable society, should not have its defects. Why are you never frank with me ?

You shall never know all the good nor all the evil in me. I have been praised all my life for qualities which I have not, and calumniated for defects which are not mine. Good-by.

XXX.

December, Monday morning.

THIS is what I call talking. To-morrow at two o'clock, where you say. I hope to see you to-morrow, delivered of your headache, in spite of which you are more amia-

4

ble than usual.   Good-by; I shall be happy
to look at the Joconde with you.

XXXI.

Wednesday.

Is it not true that the devil is painted
blacker than he is ?

XXXII.

Paris, *Sunday night, December.*

YOUR letter did not surprise me for an
instant. I expected it. I know you enough
now to be sure that whenever you have a
good thought you repent of it.   You know
very well how to gild the most bitter pills.
I owe you this justice.   As I am not the
stronger, I can say nothing against your
heroic resolution not to return to the museum.   I know very well that you will do as
you like; only I hope that before a month
from now you shall regard me more charita-
bly.   Frankly, this is what I think of you:
you like to give a vague aim to your coquetry, and that aim is I.

XXXIII.

Sunday, December 19, 1842.

THE only thing in your letter which seems clear to me is that you have a handkerchief to give to me. Send it, or tell me to come and receive it from your hand, which would be much better. I hate surprises that are announced to me, because I imagine them much more beautiful than they are in fact. Believe me, let us return to the museum together. If I bother you, that will be the end of it; if not, what prevents our meeting from time to time ?

XXXIV.

December, 1842.

Do you know that if we continue to write to each other in this tone of amiable confidence, keeping to ourselves our secret thoughts, we have only one resource; that is, to polish our style, then to publish some day our correspondence, as was done for Voiture and Balzac.

XXXV.

December, 1842.

I HAVE spent several days in bed meditating on the things of this world. I
seemed to be on the declivity of a mountain which I had climbed with much fatigue
and some amusement. This declivity was
very rough and very annoying. The only
consolation which I discovered was a little
sunlight at a great distance, a few months
spent in Italy, in Spain, or in Greece, in
oblivion of the entire world, the present
and the future.

XXXVI.

Tuesday night, December, 1842.

THERE was something in your letter of
to-day, among a lot of harsh things and of
sombre, cold thoughts, something which is
true: " I think that I never loved you so
much as yesterday." You might have
added: " I love you less to-day." I am
sure that if you were to-day as you were

yesterday, you would be full of remorse, which hardly ever troubles you.

XXXVII.

PARIS, *January* 3, 1843.

YOU are so amiable when you wish to be! Why do you choose so often to be wicked? I dined with Rachel a few days ago at an Academician's. It was to introduce Béranger to her. There were many great men there. She came late and her entrance displeased me. The men said so many silly things to her, and the women did so many silly things when they saw her, that I stayed in my corner. After dinner, Béranger, with his usual common sense, told her that it was wrong of her to waste her time in the drawing-rooms. Mademoiselle Rachel approved, and, in order to show that she heeded, she played the first act of *Esther*. She needed an assistant, and Racine's book was brought to me. I said, brutally, that I did not understand verses, and that there were people in the parlor who could scan them better than I. Hugo excused himself because of his eyes, another poet because of something else. The host devoted himself. Represent to yourself Rachel in black, between a piano and a tea-table, with a door behind her, making her theatrical face.

During the intermission, Hugo and Thiers disputed about Racine. Hugo said that Racine had a small mind, and Corneille a great one. "You say this," replied Thiers, "because you have a great mind; you are the Corneille of an epoch wherein Racine is the Casimir Delavigne." I leave you to think if modesty reigned.

XXXVIII.

Thursday, January, 1843.

WHERE you say, to-day. I suppose that you really desire to go on this promenade, for your letter is colder than the preceding ones. There is an admirable equilibrium in your manner. You do not wish me to be ever perfectly contented and you seem to take your measures in advance in order that I should be in a rage. I send you Dickens's sketches.

Perhaps you have read them, but it doesn't matter.   At two o'clock, to-day, Thursday.

XXXIX.

PARIS, *Sunday, January* 16, 1843.

I REGRET having insisted so much to make you come out in this frightful rain. It seldom happens that I sacrifice others to myself, and when it does happen I am as full of remorse as possible.   Well, you are not ill and you are not angry; that is the most important consideration.   A little misfortune comes from time to time in order to turn out a big one.   It seems to me that we were sad, although happy enough in the depths of our hearts.   There are intimate joys which may not be expressed.   I desire that you should have felt some of the sentiments which impressed me.   Good-night.

XL.

Sunday night, January, 1843.

I WAS not tired, and yet when I looked at the map of our peregrinations, I see that we

should have been both worn out. The reason is that happiness gives me strength;
from you it takes strength. I dined out,
and went to a dance afterward. I went to
sleep very late thinking of our promenade.
You made fun of me and took for a bad
compliment what I said one day of the
sleepiness, or, rather, of the torpor, which
seizes one too happy to find words to ex-
press one's emotions. I noticed yesterday
that you were under the influence of that
sleepiness. I might have reproached you in
my turn with your own reproaches; but I
was too happy to disturb my happiness.
Good-by, dear friend.

XLI.

Wednesday night, January, 1843.

I AM very susceptible to your threats.
Although I fear them, I cannot forbear to
tell you all that I think. Nothing would be
easier for me than to make promises to you,
but I feel that it would be impossible for
me to keep them. Content yourself, therefore, with our past manner of being, or let

us cease from seeing each other. I must
tell you that your insistence in opposing me
for my " frivolities " renders them dearer to
me and makes me attach greater importance
to them.   It is the only proof which you
may give me of your sentiments for me.   If
I must see you in order to resist the most
innocent temptations, this is a saint's labor
which surpasses my strength.   I should
have doubtless a great deal of pleasure in
seeing you, but the condition to transform
myself into a statue is unbearable to me.

We have made our explanations to each
other very clearly. You shall decide according to your wisdom whether we must post-
pone our next promenade to several years
from now or to the first day of sunlight.
You see that I do not accept the advice of
hypocrisy which you give me. The only
hypocrisy of which I am capable is to conceal from the people I love all the harm that
they do me.   I can sustain this effort for a
little time, but not for always.

XLII.

January, 1843.

I AM not surprised that you learned German so quickly; you possess the genius of that language, for you write in French phrases worthy of John Paul. You say, for example, " My malady is an impression of happiness which is almost a suffering." In prose this means, I hope: " I am cured and was not very ill."

You were speaking the other day of a surprise which you would make to me. Frankly, how do you want me to believe you? All that you can do is to yield when you have reached the end of your bad reasons not to yield. But how could you invent a gift when your genius is to refuse? I am very sure, for example, that you will never imagine a day for us to go out walking. Will you have Monday or Tuesday? The sky fills me with anxiety; I rely, however, on my good demon, as the Greeks say. Good-by; do not have second thoughts, and give me a place in your first thoughts.

XLIII.

PARIS, *January* 21, 1843.

IF I had seen you writing I would have divined probably from your expression what you intended to say. You are a coquette in writing, a coquette of obscurity. Alas, you think me more learned than I am in matters of dress. I have, however, fixed ideas on the subject. I will submit them to you if you wish, but I do not understand most of the beautiful things that one should admire, unless they are demonstrated to me; if you explain I will understand at once. When and how ? These two questions preoccupy me more than you think.

Have you not regretted a little the beautiful days spent under the sun of spring ?

XLIV.

January 27, 1843.

I WOULD prefer to think you cross rather than ill. If you are well and in good humor, and the weather is fine Saturday, why

should we not go out walking ? We could
go out of the world and talk. If you cannot or will not come Saturday, I shall not
be angry; but come soon. When I ask you
for anything you do it only after having
made me rage for a long time, so that you
prevent me from feeling as much gratitude
as I should, perhaps. You deprive yourself of all the merit which you would have
in being promptly generous.

XLV.

PARIS, *February* 3, 1843.

DOES not this beautiful weather make you
think of Versailles, and consequently does
it not make you feel like laughing ? If you
were logical you would not laugh. You are
not ignorant of the fact that Versailles is
the capital of the department of Seine-et-
Oise, where there are authorities for the pro-
tection of the feeble and where the language
is French. In such a land you should be as
safe as in Paris. Moreover, our aim is to
walk without running the risk of meeting

gadabouters who know us.   At Versailles,
on days when the museum is closed, we are
sure of meeting nobody.   I shall say nothing
of the air nor of the beauty of the grounds,
which have their merit, and which have an
influence always on the nature of ideas.
Think of me a little.

XLVI.

PARIS, *February* 7, 1843.

YOU are wrong to accuse me of being
fond of society; in a fortnight, I went out
only once at night to call on my minister.
I found all the women in mourning, several
of them wearing mantillas; no, not mantillas, but black beards which made them
resemble Spanish women.   It was very
pretty.   I am strangely sad and sullen.   I
wish I could quarrel with you, but I do not
know what to quarrel about.   You ought to
write me some very amiable things.   Good-
by.   I have reopened my letter in order to
pray you to observe that the weather is
better.

XLVII.

PARIS, *Sunday, February* 11, 1843.

AMONG all the amiable things that you write to me I think I discern the fact that you are not anxious to see me. Am I mistaken, or is it because I am so little accustomed to your sweetness that I cannot believe it real? Tuesday shall you be cured, shall you be free, shall you be in as good humor as last Wednesday?

XLVIII.

February 11, 1843.

THIS note takes upon itself the task of saying no, without your intervention. This ought to cure you of your bad habit of negation. The devil is bad enough without you. You gain a great deal by going out walking with me; you gain an air of health and of strength. I say nothing of the variety of information which you acquire without trouble. Now you are past mistress on the subjects of vases and statues. Every

time we meet there is a crust of ice to be
broken between us.   It is only after a quarter of an hour that we take up our last talk
at the point where we left it.   If we saw
each other oftener there would be no ice at
all.   What do you like better, the end or
the beginning of our meetings ?

XLIX.

February 17, 1843.

PERHAPS you ought to give me credit for
all my efforts to resemble you.   I cannot
understand your attitude toward me to-day.
Anyhow, I have noticed for a long time that
you love me better from afar.   But let us
not talk of this now.   I wish to say to you
only that I make no reproaches to you, that
I am not displeased with you, and if I am
at times sad, it does not mean that I am
angry.   You have made me a promise, you
know that I will not forget it.   I do not
know if I will remind you of it.   There is
nothing I detest so much as quarrelling, and
I should have to quarrel in order to give
you memory.   I wish that you should think

a little of me, and especially that we should think together. Good-by; I am charmed that the pins have pleased you. I feared you might disdain them; but despite the pleasure which I would have to see you wear them, do not put on the blue shawl. You have said sensibly that it is too showy.

L.

PARIS, *Monday night, February,* 1843.

Is it not a great folly on your part to wish to appoint fixed dates for our promenades, as if we could ever be sure of a day ? Was I not right in saying: as often as you can ? We must always suppose when there are two days of fine weather, that there shall be two months of rain afterward. You made all sorts of thoughts come to me last night at the opera, with your rainbow-colored costume. But you need not be so coquettish with me. I do not love you better in rainbow than in black.

I know the superstition about knives and sharp instruments, but not the superstition about pins. I would have thought, on the

contrary, that pins were emblems of attachment. That is why I selected them. Do
you remember that you would not let me
pick up yours ? This is one of my griev-
ances against you. I forgive them all to-
day, but I will find them all as revolting as
when they occurred when you shall have
added others to them. It is a great misfortune not to be able to forget.

LI.

Thursday night, February, 1843.

I HAVE burned your letter, but I recall it
only too distinctly. It was very sensible,
perhaps too sensible, but it was very tender
too. I have been for a week so anxious to
see you that I regret now even our quarrels.
I am writing to you; do you know why ?
In order to get angry because you will not
answer, and anything is better than the
discouragement in which you have left me.
Nothing is more absurd; we were right to
say farewell. You and I understand so well
reasonable things that we should act most
reasonably. But there is happiness only in

folly and dreams.   I never believed before
that our quarrels could endure.   But it is
ten days now since we parted in a manner
almost solemn, which has frightened me.
Were we more angry than usual, did we
love each other less ?   There was between
us that day certainly something which I
cannot recall distinctly, but which had not
existed before.   Little accidents come after
big ones.   Good-by; answer me.

LII.

Thursday morning, February, 1843.

HAVE you reflected on the fact that it is
an admirable invention to place in a beautiful palace pictures and statues, and let people walk among them ?   Unfortunately, this
beautiful place is to be closed.   Are you
not sorry ?   Believe me, let us say good-by
together to all these old statues.   Saturday
is an admirable day, for only Englishmen
come then, and they are not troublesome to
those who like to look at pictures.   What
think you of Saturday, that is, after to-mor-

row ? It will be the last Saturday. This
word " last " grieves me. Then, Saturday, I
will wait for you at two o'clock in front of
the Joconde, unless the weather be horrible.

Why do you use paper so small, and why
do you write to me only three lines, two of
which are to quarrel with me ? What matters it if one live faster, provided one live hap-
pier ? Is it not better to have reminiscences
than years which one cannot remember ?

LIII.

Paris, *February*, 1843.

Do you not admire, as I do, that strange
coincidence—I shall not say sympathy, I do
not wish to displease you—of our thoughts ?
Do you remember that formerly we made
an experiment almost as miraculous, and
recently, near a stove in the Spanish Museum, you read in my mind as quickly as I
thought ? I have suspected for some time
that there was something diabolical in you.
I am reassured when I think that I saw your
two feet. They are not cloven. Yet you

might have hidden from me a small hoof
under your boots. Pray reassure me.
Good-by.

LIV.

PARIS, *February* 19, 1843.

FORTUNATELY it is the post-office which
made me wait so long for your letter. Although I suffered from this tardiness, I did
not accuse you for a single moment. I am
glad to say this to you in order that you may
know that I am curing myself of my faults,
as you are of yours.

LV.

PARIS, *February* 27, 1843.

THE verb of which you are so much afraid
has always a very sweet sound, even if it
be accompanied by all the adverbs which
you know so well how to twist around it.
You frightened me, dear friend, when you
said that you dared not write, and that you
would have no longer the courage to speak.
You say the reverse of this when we are

together. Will not the result be that you will neither speak nor write to me? You were angry with me, you said. Was it just, and had I deserved it? Had I not your promise? I am beginning to know you, and that is, I think, what saddens me so often. There is in you a mixture of oppositions and of contradictions so strange that it would enrage a saint.

LVI.

Thursday, March 1, 1843.

SATURDAY, then. It is a long time since we have had a quarrel. Do you not think it preferable rather than our anger of former times? You still have a defect: that of making yourself so scarce. We see each other hardly once in a fortnight. Each time there is a new crust of ice to be broken. I am to you like an old opera which you need to forget in order to see again with pleasure. I, on the contrary, would love you more if I saw you more. Prove to me that I am wrong, and appoint a day when I can see you soon.

LVII.

PARIS, *Friday morning, March* 13, 1843.

HERE is your cravat. It was found Saturday in the antechamber of His Royal Highness Monseigneur le Duc de Nemours. Nobody asked for an explanation of its presence in my pocket. I would have sent it sooner if I had not wished to add the desire of regaining your property to that of your sending news of yourself to me. I perceive that although the first desire was very vivid in you it could not triumph over the indifference of your second desire. Why are you so afraid of the cold ? Reply quickly.

LVIII.

PARIS, *March* 14, 1843.

IT is a crime not to take advantage of the beautiful weather. What think you of a walk to-morrow, Thursday ? You should be the first to speak of it, but you do not. We must go to salute the first leaves. I think also of the influence which the sun-

light has on your humor. I should like to
try it. I love you in all sorts of weather.
Good-by.

LIX.

PARIS, *Saturday night, March*, 1843.

NOT the least trace of repentance in your
letter. I regret the amber pipe which you
had selected. There is something particularly agreeable in carrying often to my mouth
a gift from you. But let it be as you
wish. I say this very often, and always without reward for my resignation. I envy the
fate of women, who have nothing to do but
to make themselves beautiful and prepare
for the effect which they want to produce
upon others. Others is an ugly word, but it
preoccupies you more than me. I am very
angry with you without knowing the cause
of it; but there must be a real cause, for I
could not be in the wrong. It seems to me
that you become more selfish day by day.
In " us " you find only " you." The more I
think of this the sadder it is. We are so different that we can hardly understand each

other.   Good-by.   I hope to see you Tuesday.   I hope to see you in a better humor.

LX.

Monday night, March 21, 1843.

IF I have pained you I am as repentant as
I can be, but I hope that I have not given you
as much pain as I felt.   You have often reproached me for being indifferent; I suppose you meant only that I was not demon-
strative.   When I am not myself, the reason
is that I suffer much.   Admit that after so
long an acquaintance with me it is sad to
think that you mistrust me.   Good-by.   No
more quarrels.   I shall try to be more reasonable.

LXI.

March, 1843.

I WAS as tired as if I had walked four or
five leagues, but the fatigue was so agreeable
that I would like to feel it again.   All was
so successful that although I am accustomed to the success of a well-laid plan, I
share your astonishment.   To be so free and

so far away from the world, is it not amusing? Do you know why I took only one flower from that bunch of hyacinths so pretty and so white? The reason is that I wished to keep some for another occasion. You ask if I believe in the soul. Not too much. Nevertheless, when I reflect upon certain things, I find an argument in favor of that hypothesis. Here it is: How could two inanimate substances give and receive a sensation through a union which would be insipid were it not for the idea that is attached to it? This is a very pedantic phrase to say that when two people who love each other kiss each other they feel something else than the sensation of kissing the softest satin. But the argument has its value. We shall talk of metaphysics if you wish next time. It is a subject which I like a great deal because one may not exhaust it.

LXII.

Friday, March 29, 1843.

IF you knew how sweet you were the other day you would never consent to be

vexing, as you are sometimes. I would have
liked you to be still more frank; nevertheless, it seemed as if your thoughts were all
revealed to me, although your phrases were
more complicated than the Apocalypse.   I
wish you had a hundredth part of the pleasure which I feel in seeing you think.   There
are two persons in you.   The better one is
all heart and all soul.   The other is a pretty
statue well polished by fashion, well draped
in silk and cashmere; a charming automaton,
the springs of which are skilfully arranged.
When one imagines that he is talking to
the first he is talking to the statue.   Why
should that statue be so pretty ?

LXIII.

Friday night, April 8th.

I HAVE had a horrible headache for two
days, and you write me all sorts of wicked
things.   The worst is that you have no remorse, and I hoped that you would have
some.   I am so downhearted that I have
not the strength even to scold you.   What

is the miracle of which you are talking?
The only possible miracle would be to make
you less stubborn, and I will never achieve
that. It is too far beyond my power. I
shall have to wait, therefore, until Monday
to guess the enigma.

Your idea from Wilhelm Meister is pretty
enough, but it is only a sophism after all.
One might say with as much exactness that
the memory of a pleasure is a variety of
sorrow. That is true, especially of half
pleasures. I mean those which are not
shared. You shall have your portrait in
Turkish dress. I placed a narghile in your
hand for local color. When I say that you
shall have it, I mean if you pay. If you
are not graceful about it I shall revenge
myself terribly. Somebody asked me to-
day for a drawing for an album which is to
be sold in the interest of the earthquake's
victims, and I will give your portrait.

LXIV.

PARIS, *April* 15, 1843.

YOU do not comprehend my generosity in sacrificing myself to you. You ought to thank me in order to encourage me. But you believe that all is due to you. Why is it that we agree so rarely in our points of view? You did well not to talk of Catullus. He is not an author that one should read in Passion week. One sees very well in his work what love was in Rome fifty years before Christ. It was a little better than love at Athens in the time of Pericles. Already women were something. They made men do silly things. Their power came, I think, not from Christianity, as it is usual to say, but through the influence which the barbarians of the North exercised on Roman society. The Germans were exalted. They liked minds. The Romans cared only for the body. It is true that for a long time women had no minds. They have not any now in the Orient, and it is a great pity. You know how two minds talk to each other. But yours hardly listens to mine.

LXV.

PARIS, *May* 4, 1843.

I CANNOT sleep at all and am in a dog's humor. Your distinction between the two " Ego " is very pretty. It proves your profound selfishness. You love only yourself, and that is why you love a little the Ego which resembles yours. It scandalized me often day before yesterday. I was thinking of it sadly while you were preoccupied by nothing but contemplating the trees in your own way. Every time we see each other you are armed with an envelope of ice which melts only after a quarter of an hour. At my return, you shall have amassed a veritable iceberg. Well, it is better not to think of evil before it occurs. Let us dream always.

LXVI.

Wednesday, June, 1843.

WHY should we not see each other Friday? If it should not inconvenience you, I would have the greatest pleasure. I hope that the weather will be fine. You promised to tell me something which must be too im-

portant to be postponed.   I will take a Spanish book and we will read, if you wish.   You
have not said if you would pay for my lessons.   The time not spent in telling what
you call silly things seems to me to be so
badly spent that I ought at least to earn
something.   Could I not give you Spanish
lessons at your house?   I would call myself
Don Furlano and would have a letter of introduction to you from one of your friends
who would describe me as a victim of Espartero's tyranny.

I am beginning to find unbearable our de-
pendence on sunlight and rain.   You promise often to invent something.   You pretend
to govern, but in truth you do your work
badly.   I can judge only imperfectly your
possibilities and your impossibilities.   If
you meditated on the petty problem of our
seeing each other as often as possible you
would do a good act.   I have many other
things to tell you, but I should have to recall our quarrel, and I should like to annihi-
late the memory of it.   Good-by.   Think
of your statue and animate it without tor-
menting it.

LXVII.

PARIS, *June* 14, 1843.

I AM glad to learn that you are better, and very sorry that you have wept. You must understand always what I say. You see anger or wickedness where there is only sadness. I do not remember what I said to you, but I am sure that I wished to say nothing save that you had grieved me a great deal. All the quarrels which occur between us prove to me that we are very different, and as there is a great affinity between us in spite of this difference, there results necessarily a struggle which makes me suffer. When I tell you that I suffer, it is not a reproach that I am addressing to you.

Your system of government is always the same; you will always make me rage after having made me very happy at times. Somebody who is more philosophical than I would take the happiness when it comes, and not worry about the unhappiness. It is the fault of my temperament to recall all the evil that has passed when I am suffer-

ing. But I recall also all the happiness
when I am happy.

LXVIII.

SINCE you did not catch cold, I can recall
with happiness all the moments we spent
together. I think, as you do, that we were
on that day more perfectly—if perfectly
admits a more or a less—happy than ever.
Why was it? We said or did nothing extraordinary. We did not quarrel. Observe,
if you please, that it is from you always
that quarrels come. I have yielded to you
on an infinity of points, and was not in a
bad humor for that.

LXIX.

YOU do well to forget quarrels if you can.
They are bigger when examined too closely.
It is better to dream as long as possible, and
as we can have always the same dream, it
resembles a reality. It is a pity that we

should not meet the day after a quarrel. I am sure that we should be perfectly amiable. You have promised to appoint a day for me, but you have not thought of it. Or you have thought that it would be an indecorous thing to do. It is that preoccupation in you which is so often a cause of quarrel between us. I may have said that you constrained yourself a great deal to please me; I am incessantly in a rage against this constraint which, even in its most agreeable element, conceals always a sad thought.

LXX.

PARIS, *July*, 1843.

I WENT to the country yesterday, and returned very tired and very sad. Tired because I was bored, and sad because I was thinking that it was a beautiful day lost. Do you ever make such a reproach to yourself? I hope not. At times I believe that you feel all that I feel; then drawbacks come, and I believe in nothing.

6

LXXI.

Thursday evening, July 28, 1843.

YOU have guessed my thoughts well enough, perhaps, but not entirely. You could never divine them all. I change them so often that what is true in one moment ceases to be true a few moments after. You are wrong to accuse yourself. You have, I think, no other reproach against yourself than those which I make to you. You are wrong to accuse me of not wanting to see you. I never said a word about it. There is another thing which we might do. Not write a word to each other during my trip, and not meet at my return. That is reasonable enough, but hard to execute. When I am not thinking of your letter, do you know what I would like ? I would like to see you once again. Perhaps you would have no objections to saying good-by to me Saturday. I am perhaps wrong to suggest this. God knows in what mood you are ! After all, you can say yes or no. I promise never to be cross again.

LXXII.

PARIS, *Thursday night, August 2*, 1843.

HOW ingenious you are in taking enchantment from others and from yourself. I say enchantment, perhaps wrongly, for I do not think that marmots have any. You were one of these pretty animals before Brahma sent your soul into a woman's body. In truth, you wake up sometimes, and, as you say yourself, to quarrel. Be good and graceful as you know how to be. In spite of my bad humor, I prefer to see you with your grand, indifferent airs, rather than not see you at all. Good-by.

LXXIII.

PARIS, *August 5*, 1843.

I WAS waiting for a letter from you with great impatience, and the more time it took to come, the more I expected evidences of second movements and their ugly consequences. As I was prepared for all sorts of insults from you, your letter seemed better

than it would have seemed in any other
moment. You say that you were happy,
too, and this word effaces all the others that
precede and follow. It is the best thing you
have said to me for a long time; it is almost
the only time when I felt that your heart was
not different from others. What a radiant
promenade!

LXXIV.

VEZELAY, *August* 8, 1843.

I THANK you for having written a word to
me before my departure. It is the intention which pleased me, not the expression of
your letter. You say extraordinary things.
If you thought half of the things that you
say, it would be wiser for us never to meet
again. Your affection for me is only a sort
of mind's play. You are one of those chilly
women of the North; you live only by the
head. What I could say to you, you would
not understand. You can divine my thoughts
sometimes, but you will never understand
them.

What is certain is, that we had formed of

each other an idea probably very different from that which we have now.   If we knew then how much we were to vex each other, do you think that we would have ever met? It is frightfully cold.   I have to write a ream of official prose, and I quit you the more easily because the things I would say to you are not full of tenderness.   I am as discontented with myself as with you.   You would be amiable if you wrote to me at Dijon.   Especially if you found under your pen something less brutal than your last letter.   At Dijon, *poste restante*, and do not forget my titles and qualities!

LXXV.

AVALLON, *August* 14, 1843.

IN general I do not like my own society; but when I am sad without good reason I am pleased by complete solitude.   I was in this mood during my last days at Vezelay.   I walked on the terrace and philosophized on the Ego and on Providence, if there be a Providence.   I thought of you also, and more agreeably than of me.   But that thought was

not the gayest, because as soon as it came
it occurred to me how happy I would be to
see you here in this unknown corner. And
then—and then all ended with this other
thought, more despairing, that you were
very far away, that it was not easy to see
you, and not certain that you would wish
to be seen.

My presence at Vezelay has mystified the
population. Considerable groups formed
themselves around me wherever I went.
This attention bored me much, and I wished
I had a janissary to disperse the curious.
Here I came to see an old uncle whom I
hardly knew. I had to remain with him for
two days. I do not like relatives. They
compel one to be familiar with people whom
one never saw. My uncle is a good man,
not too provincial, and perhaps I might
think him amiable if we had two ideas in
common. Women here are as ugly as in
Paris. Moreover, their ankles are as big as
posts.

I send you an owl's feather which I found
in a hole of the church. The former owner
of the feather and I met for an instant. We

were equally frightened by our unexpected
meeting. The owl was less brave than I,
and flew. It had a formidable bill and
frightful eyes, besides two feathers shaped
like horns. I send you this feather in order
that you should admire its softness and because I have read in a book of magic that
when a man gives to a woman an owl's
feather and she places it under her pillow
she dreams of him. Will you tell me your
dream? Good-by.

LXXVI.

SAINT-LUPICIN, *August* 15, 1843.

> Six hundred metres above the level
> of the sea. In the middle of an
> ocean of agile and famished fleas.

YOU practise the axiom that language is
given to man to conceal his thoughts. Fortunately for you, your postscriptum disarmed
me. Why do you say in German what you
think in French? Is it because you think it
in German; that is, do not think it at all? I

do not wish to believe it. But there are in
you things that irritate me extremely.

Saint-Lupicin is in the mountains of the
Jura. It is very ugly, dirty, and full of fleas.
I think often that if railways were better we
might go together to such a place and make
it beautiful. There is an immense quantity
of flowers here, and the air is so pure that
the human voice can be heard at a distance
of three miles. To prove to you that I am
thinking of you, here is a little flower which
I picked up in my walk under the setting
sun.

What are you doing? What are you
thinking of? You will never tell me what
you are thinking of really, and it is folly for
me to ask you. I cannot become accustomed to my solitude. It is more painful
this year than ever. It seems to me that if
I were in prison I would be more comfortable than I am running through the country.
I regret my walks. I have no desire to go
to Italy. It is an invention of yours. Your
letter pleased me at times, and at others en-
raged me. I read between the lines at one
moment the softest things, at other moments

only chilliness.   Nothing but the postscriptum satisfies me.   I saw it late.   It is placed
at such a great distance from the rest of the
letter!

LXXVII.

PARIS, *September*, 1843.

Is it true now that we shall not see each
other again?   We quitted each other without speaking, without looking at each other,
almost.   I felt a sort of calm happiness
which is not usual to me, the other day.   It
seemed to me for a few moments that I desired nothing more.   Now, if we can get that
happiness again, why should we refuse it? It
is true that we can quarrel again, but it has
happened so often.   What is the memory of
a quarrel in comparison with that of making
up!   If you think half as much of all this as
I do, you must be desirous of going on one
of our walks again.   Saturday, if you wish,
or Tuesday, we might meet.   I had persuaded myself that you would be the first
to talk of it.   I was mistaken.

LXXVIII.

PARIS, *September*, 1843.

YOU are wrong to repent for what you have done; I was wrong to wish you to be different. Pray believe that I have not changed. I regret having left you as I did, but there are moments when one cannot be cool. I should like to see you now in order to regain one of our beautiful dreams of this summer and say good-by to you for a long time, leaving a soft and tender impression. You will find this idea absurd. Yet it pursues me, and I cannot forbear from telling it to you. Refuse, you will do well, perhaps. I think I will have enough control over myself not to be angry. What you decide will be well. I can only promise you my best intentions to be calm and resigned.

LXXIX.

AVIGNON, *September 29th.*

IT is a long time since I have received news from you, and almost as long a time

since I have written to you. But I am ex-
cusable. My trade is most tiresome. I have
to walk or run by day and write a dozen pages
of prose by night.

The country that I am traversing is admirable, but the people in it are excessively
stupid. Nobody opens his mouth except to
praise himself. There is no appearance here
of the tact which makes the gentleman, and
which I found with so much pleasure among
the common people of Spain. Barring this,
it is impossible to see a country which resembles Spain more. The workingmen lie
down in the shade or drape themselves with
their mantles with an air as tragic as that of
the Andalusians. The odor of garlic and oil
is mingled everywhere with that of oranges
and jessamine. The streets are covered with
canvas during the day, and the women have
little, well-shod feet.

September 30*th*.—I sprained my foot last
night. I am writing to you in a state of impatience hard to describe. If I were compelled to spend five or six days more here,
I do not know what would become of me.
I think I would prefer to be seriously ill

rather than to be stopped by such a little thing.

Avignon is full of churches and palaces, all surmounted by high towers. The palace of the Popes is a model of middle-age fortification. This shows what amiable security reigned in the land in the thirteenth or fourteenth century. In the palace of the Popes you ascend a hundred steps of a tortuous stairway, then find yourself suddenly in front of a wall. You turn your head and see, fifteen feet above you, the continuation of the stairway which you cannot reach without a ladder. There are also subterranean rooms which were used by the Inquisition. They show you the furnaces where the irons were heated to torture the heretics.

LXXX.

TOULON, *October 2d.*

MY journey lengthens while the days shorten. It is impossible to see anything dirtier and prettier than Marseilles, whence I have just come. Dirty and pretty fit the women of Marseilles perfectly. All have

beautiful black eyes, beautiful teeth, small
feet and imperceptible ankles. These little
feet wear cinnamon stockings, the color of
the mud of Marseilles. Their gowns are
badly cut. Their beautiful black hair owes
the greater part of its lustre to tallow. Add
to this an atmosphere of garlic mingled with
rancid oil vapor, and you may represent to
yourself the beauty of Marseilles. What a
pity it is that there should be nothing perfect in the world ! Well, the Marseilles
women are ravishing in spite of everything.
I need a letter from you to reanimate me.

LXXXI.

Paris, *Friday morning, November* 3, 1843.

What is it that prevents you from being
frank, and makes you seek for the most extraordinary lies in order to conceal a word
of truth which would please me so much ?
Among the good sentiments of which you
speak there is one, you say, which I do not
understand ; and as you do not try to make me
understand it, I cannot even divine it. As
for the two others, I am not more skilful.

Do you believe in the devil? If he frightens you, take care that he does not carry you away. If the devil has nothing to do with the case, as I imagine, there remains the question whether one harms anybody. I tell you my catechism. I have never tried to convert any one, but no one has been able to convert me. You address to me reproaches much more severe than those which I make to you. Sometimes I yield to sadness and to impatience. I charge you with nothing except that lack of frankness which places me in an attitude of mistrust almost continual, forced as I am to seek for your thought under a disguise. If I were convinced of what you said the other day, I would be very miserable, for I could not endure grieving you. I do not know what your thoughts are, what your sentiments are; write to me frankly at least once.

LXXXII.

PARIS, *November* 16, 1843.

YOU were so good and so graceful that I would forgive you, I think, a return to bad humor, provided you said your walk did you no harm. I slept all day, in this half somnolence that you like. If I were not accustomed to think aloud in your presence, I should be almost tempted to be angry always, for you are so amiable then that one may not repent for having caused you grief. However, I recall only the moments when we had the same thoughts and when it seemed to me that you forgot my importunity and my conceit. I suppose that you enjoyed yourself at your ball yesterday.

LXXXIII.

PARIS, *Tuesday night, November* 22, 1843.

IT is difficult for me to think that your stubbornness is involuntary. Even if it were, you would be in the wrong. What is the result of it ? By giving with bad grace you deprive of merit the sacrifice which you are making. You feel the pain of this sacrifice the more because you have not the consolation to think that the merit of it is appreciated. To speak as you do, you give me double remorses. I have told you this more than once. You judge me badly. It is true that we have different temperaments and can never judge of things in the same manner. How do you want me to quarrel on the subject: " Who loves the better ? " The first thing to do would be to agree on the meaning of the verb, and that we never shall.

It is better for us to quarrel than not to meet. This seems to me to be proved. When shall we quarrel ?

LXXXIV.

PARIS, *December* 13, 1843.

WE quitted each other in anger; but when I reflect calmly upon it, I regret nothing that I said, unless it be the vivacity of several words, for which I beg your pardon. We should have seen sooner how contrary were our sentiments about everything. The concessions which we made to each other had no other result than to make us more miserable. I have made you suffer a great deal in order to prolong an illusion which I should not have conceived.

Forgive me, I pray you, for I have suffered like you. I wish I could leave you better memories of me. I hope that you will attribute to circumstances the sorrow which I may have caused you. I was never with you as I would have liked to have been, or rather, as I wish to appear to you. I have had too much confidence in myself. Perhaps you will care to recollect only the happy moments which were passed in each other's company. I cannot reproach you for anything. You have tried to reconcile two incompatible things and you have not succeeded. Must I not give you credit for having tried in my favor to do the impossible ?

LXXXV.

PARIS, *Tuesday night*, 1844.

THE clouds played a great part, perhaps, in what happened between us. Once before, we quarrelled in stormy weather; this is because our nerves are stronger than we. I wish to see you and to know how you are morally. What do you think of making to-morrow the promenade which we missed

7

yesterday ? Your pride will say no, but I
am appealing to your heart.

LXXXVI.

PARIS, *Saturday night, January* 15, 1844.

I AM sorry that you are ill.   But you will
permit me to believe only what I can believe
of the manner of your catching cold.   This
accident seldom keeps one in bed; still more
seldom does it keep one in bed as long as
it keeps you.   All your illnesses have happened too opportunely not to be a little
suspicious to me.   Formerly you were more
frank.   You simply wrote a page of reproaches and said that you were angry.
Now you have another system.   You write
little notes which are very pretty and coquettish and say that you are ill or that you
have a cold.   I think I preferred your
other process.   I hope to meet you in better humor Tuesday.   You treat me like the
sun, which comes out only once a month.
Good-by; I am not very well pleased with
you.   A month without seeing you is too
long.

LXXXVII.

YOU reproach me for my harshness, and, perhaps, with some reason. It seems to me, however, that it would be more just to say anger or impatience. It might be well enough on your part to think whether this anger or this harshness be natural, or not.

Examine if it be not sad for me to find myself incessantly at war with your conceit and to see that it has the preference. I confess that I understand not at all what you say of your obedience, which puts you in the wrong in everything and gives you the merit of nothing. But you are neither wrong nor meritorious. Recall for a moment with frankness what you are to me. You accept these promenades which are my life; but the coldness which makes me despair more and more, the pleasure which you have in making me desire what you refuse obstinately, may excuse my harshness. Your pride is only a variety of selfishness. Will you put aside some day

this great defect and be to me as amiable
as you can ? Good-by.

LXXXVIII.

PARIS, *March* 12, 1844.

NEXT Thursday, at one o'clock, I shall be
again an ordinary biped; is it too much to
expect of you that you shall send me a few
tender words ?

LXXXIX.

Thursday night, March 15, 1844.

MY election as a member of the French
Academy has pleased me because I expected
to be defeated. My mother, who had been
suffering from rheumatism, was cured at
once. The greater is my desire to see you.
Come and see if I love you more or less, as
soon as you can.

XC.

March 17, 1844.

I THANK you for your compliments, but
I want more. I want to see you. Why do

you weep ? The forty seats of the French
Academy were not worth a small tear.
There were members who blackballed me
seven times and who say now that they were
my warmest partisans. At least you and I
are sure of each other, and when you tell
me untruths I can reproach you for them,
and you know how to get forgiveness for
them. Love me, venerable as I am.

XCI.

PARIS, *March* 26, 1844.

I FEAR that my discourse may have seemed
to you long. I hope it was not as cold in
your corner as in mine. I am still shiver-
ing. We should have taken a short walk together after the ceremony. Did you like
the orator better in his costume ? Good-
by; I was very glad to see you. I had
much trouble to find you hidden behind
your neighbor's bonnet.

XCII.

Thursday night, March, 1844.

WHY should there be pride, that is selfishness, between us ? You were so amiable this morning that I do not wish to quarrel with you. Yet I am in a terrible humor. I do not know if it would be well for you to go out to-morrow; I fear the responsibility of giving you advice on that point, and prefer that you should decide. Observe my humility.

XCIII.

STRASBURG, *April* 30, 1844.

I SPENT a day delivering the most sublime eloquence to make the municipal council restore an old church. They say that they need tobacco more than monuments and will make a shop of my church. I am glad to find you so joyful. I am in a horrible humor. The cathedral which I loved appears ugly to me. You are right to like Paris. It is, after all, the only city where

one may live.   I would like to believe in
your promise, but I know what to expect.
Thick ice shall have been formed between us.
You will not even recognize me.   Good-by.

XCIV.

PARIS, *Saturday, August* 3, 1844.

I SUPPOSE that you went to the country,
taking French leave in spite of your promise.
That is very amiable of you.   I was naïve
enough to expect something from you.   It
is hard for one to change.   I have to go out
of town for a month or two.   If this gave
you remorse, or, better, the desire to see me,
you might make me forget my bad humor.

XCV.

PARIS, *August* 19, 1844.

I SHALL not see you before January.
You should have thought of that before
your departure.   When I say that you shall
not see me until next year, I mean that it
depends on you.   While you are learning
Greek, I am studying Arabic.   It is a dia-

bolical language and I will never know two words of it. I went to dinner Sunday with General Narvaez. There were only Spanish women. One of them is trying to starve herself for love and is dying slowly. This mode of death will impress you as very cruel. Good-by.

XCVI.

PARIS, *Monday, September*, 1844.

IT is evident that we cannot meet now without quarrelling. We want the impossible: you, that I should be a statue; I, that you should not be one. Every new proof of this impossibility is cruel for both of us. I regret all the grief that I have caused you. I yield too often to my absurd impatience. I might as well be angry because ice is cold.

I hope that you forgive me now; I feel no anger, but much sadness. Good-by, since we can be friends only at a distance. When we are old, perhaps we shall meet again with pleasure. Meanwhile, in happiness or unhappiness, remember me.

XCVII.

PARIS, *Thursday, September* 6, 1844.

WE spent so little time together that I told you nothing that I wished to say. It seems to me that I saw you in a dream. You had not the air of knowing that I was a reality. When shall we meet again ?

XCVIII.

PARIS, *September* 14, 1844.

I AM not going to Africa. I shall be out of town for a fortnight and return then to Paris. I regard this change with impassibility. Perhaps you can guess why.

I do not see how you spend the twenty-four hours of the day. I know how you use sixteen of them, but I want details on eight. Do you read Herodotus ? Good-by.

XCIX.

POITIERS, *September* 15, 1844.

YOU let ten entire days pass without writing a line to me, and it is very wicked

of you. I believe that you have enjoyed
yourself a great deal and I cannot forbear
from thinking that you enjoy yourself only
when you have the occasion to be a coquette.
I have led a very dull life since my departure
from Paris. Like Ulysses I have seen many
manners, men and things. Your memory
represents itself to me now in a multitude
of places, but I ally it specially with woods
and with museums. If you derive some
pleasure from occupying a place in my
memory you must think that I am not forgetting you. I spend my time meditating
on our promenades.

C.

PARTHENAY, *September* 17, 1844.

APPARENTLY I shall be in Paris before
you. To be there without you will seem
harder to me than to be running through
the fields as I am doing at present. I wish
to see you with an ardor which you cannot
understand. Will you deign to come ? I
try not to think of it, but cannot succeed.
In order to be prepared for my deceptions I

try to represent to myself your ladyship as
a statue with a cuirass.   Good-by.

CI.

PERPIGNAN, *November 14th.*

I HAVE been tormented by an absurd idea
which I dared not tell you.   I was visiting
the arena at Nîmes with an architect of
the department who was explaining to me
at length the repairs which he had ordered,
when I saw at a distance of ten steps from
me a charming bird with a linen-gray body
and wings red, black, and white.   This bird
was perched on a cornice and looked at me
fixedly.   I interrupted the architect to ask
him the name of the bird.   He is a great
sportsman and yet he had never seen a bird
like it.   I went near it and it flew when I
tried to touch it.   It stood a few steps fur-
ther, still gazing at me.   Wherever I went
it followed me.   Its flight was noiseless like
that of a nocturnal bird.

I returned to the arena the next day and
saw the bird again.   I had brought bread
which I threw at it.   It looked at it but

would not touch it. I threw a big cricket, thinking from the form of the bird's bill that it ate insects, but it did not care for the cricket. The most learned ornithologist of the city told me that there were no birds of that species in the land. At my last visit to the arena I met my bird, forever attached to my steps, to such an extreme that it went with me into a narrow and dark corridor where, being a day bird, it should not have come. I remembered then that the Duchess of Buckingham had seen her husband in the form of a bird the day of his assassination, and the idea came to me that you were, perhaps, dead and that you had taken this form to see me. In spite of me, this silly idea annoyed me, and I assure you that I was enchanted to see your letter bearing the date of the day when I saw for the first time my marvellous bird. I am writing to you from a small room which is very cold. The servant talks only Catalonian and understands me only when I speak in Spanish. I have not a book and know nobody. I went to the fountain of Vaucluse, where I had a great wish to inscribe your name; but there were so many bad verses, so many Sophies and Carolines that I did not wish to put your name in such bad company. It is a very savage place. There are only water and rocks. The vegetation is reduced to a fig tree which grew, I know not how, among the stones, and two very elegant capillary plants, a sample of which I send you. If I do not find a letter from you at Toulouse I shall be mortally angry with you. Good-by.

CII.

PARIS, *December* 5, 1844.

I HAD sworn not to write to you, but I do not think I could have kept my promise much longer. I did not think that you were ill. Our promenade had been so joyful! I did not think it possible that you might have a bad remembrance of it. Seemingly, what irritates you is my being more stubborn than you. That is a good reason of which you should be glorious. I think, however, that you should be ashamed of yourself for having made me so. And then you say that I was harsh with you and you ask if I did not realize it. Frankly, no. Why did you not tell me if I was? If I was, I beg your pardon. It seems to me that we parted without any expression of grief from you. I thought you were as confident, as intimate, as I was to you. If you were angry, that does honor to your dissimulation. I shall bring to you the sketch which I have made and also your portrait. I have painted your angry eyes. Do not believe that this is their ordinary expression. I know a better one. When you pay me, please recollect that I am not an ordinary painter. It is not the work which you are to pay for, but the trouble and the time. Then, it is well always to be generous with artists.

CIII.

PARIS, *Thursday, February* 7, 1845.

IT was better than I expected. I spoke at the Academy with rare calmness. I do not know if my audience liked me, but I liked it.

CIV.

Friday, February 8, 1845.

SINCE you did not think me ridiculous all is well. Why not to-morrow? Otherwise we should have to wait till Wednesday and I have not the courage. We have so many things to say to each other.

CV.

TOULOUSE, *August* 18, 1845.

YOU shall say that I was wrong to expect you to think of me sooner than you have. I cannot become accustomed to your ways. You are never so near forgetting me as when you have persuaded me that you are thinking of me. I should like to spoil you as you desire, but I am in too bad a humor. I have spent a day at a deputy's, and if I had the ambition to be a politician that visit would have made me change my mind. I prefer the court of a despot rather than the house of a deputy. Most despots wash their hands.

I would like to think that yours will be the
first friendly face that shall present itself to
me in Paris at my return. Unfortunately
it shall not be, and you shall wait until the
trees are leafless to return to Paris. Who
knows if you will not return as an English
woman ? Promise me that this shall not be,
that you shall not remain away too long and
that you shall not be worse than you are.

CVI.

AVIGNON, *September* 5, 1845.

I AM troubled with dizziness. While you
are eating melting peaches I am eating yellow ones, very tart and singular in taste. I
am eating figs of all colors. I am horribly
bothered at night and regret the society of
bipeds like me. I do not regard the provin-
cials as anybody. They are things very tiresome to my eyes and foreign to the circle of
my ideas. These southerners are strange
people: at times I think they are witty, at
others I think they have only vivacity.

CVII.

BARCELONA, *November* 10, 1845.

MY apartment recalls to my mind the cara-
vansaries of Asia. It is more comfortable
here than in Andalusia, but the natives are
inferior to the Andalusians.

CVIII.

MADRID, *November* 18, 1845.

THANKS to the extreme slowness of the
people of this country, I began only to-day
to read the manuscripts which I came to
consult. An academic deliberation was
necessary to permit me to examine them,
and I cannot tell you the number of intrigues
which were indispensable in order to obtain
information of their existence.

This country has changed a great deal
since my last visit. Those whom I left
friends have become mortal enemies. Many
of my former acquaintances have become
great lords, and very insolent. Here people
talk aloud. Their frankness is very surpris-
ing, especially to me, whom you have accus-

8

tomed to something else. You should go to the other side of the Pyrenees in order to take a lesson in veracity.

In spite of your infernal coquetry and of your aversion to the truth, I like you better than all the frank persons whom I meet here. Do not take advantage of this avowal. Good-by.

CIX.

PARIS, *Monday, January* 19, 1846.

YOU do not tell me the thing which would interest me most; that is, when I may see you. This proves that you have no desire to see me. Do you wish to walk out Wednesday ? If you have the toothache, do not come. If you have any other malady I shall admit of no excuse, for I will not believe in it.

CX.

PARIS, *June* 10, 1846.

YOU are never so near being bad to me as when you have just been kind and graceful. You had promised to appoint a day soon. But if I waited for you to keep your promises

the patience which Heaven gave me would
not suffice. The other day you were as
indifferent in saying good-by to me as in
greeting me. You were not thus the previous time. It is a curious phenomenon
that water which has been boiled freezes
more easily than cold water. You are an
illustration of that experiment in physics.
When you quitted me you had your pouting
attitude, so I expect that you shall be charming Wednesday. You will please me greatly
by coming. But pleasing me does not affect
you much. I will give you something. At
least, I wish to give you something, but you
have been so cruel to me that I do not know
if I will give it to you. Still, if you ask for
it, it is probable that I will yield.

CXI.

Dijon, *July* 29, 1846.

I EXPECTED to find a letter from you here,
but suppose you are enjoying yourself too
much to think of writing to me. What are
you doing, where are you ? I have the
spleen, perhaps because you have forgotten

me. Why did you not write to me? I
have reason to be furious.

CXII.

August 10, 1846.
On board a steamer, the name
of which I do not know.

ALTHOUGH you have given me the habit
of your negligence toward me, I cannot re-
frain from being anxious when I have no
news from you. I wish you would deign to
think of me as often as I think of you. I
do not doubt that you will enjoy yourself
a great deal where you are going, but if,
among your pleasures, the remembrance of
our promenades should come to you, you
would do a meritorious act by hastening
your return.

CXIII.

PARIS, *August* 18, 1846.

AT my return here I feel more isolated and
sadder than in any of the cities which I have
quitted. I feel like an emigrant who returns
to his country and finds in it a new genera-

tion. Alas! What I say will not make
you return an hour sooner. I should be
wiser to be resigned. When your gowns
shall have faded in the sea air, perhaps you
will think of me, but then I shall be at
Cologne, or perhaps at Barcelona. They
say that for a woman nothing is so agreeable as to show pretty gowns. I cannot
offer to you joys equivalent to that.

CXIV.

Paris, *August* 22, 1846.

BEFORE your departure you seemed to be
in a great hurry to see me. I have com-
plained for a long time between " saying "
and " doing " in you. You spend your time so
happily, so agreeably, that you do not think,
even, of your return to Paris. You ask if it
would please me, which is wicked derision.
I am even lonelier here than when I travelled,
and yet am busy enough not to regret the
absence of people from Paris; but I do not
care for them. It is our walks that I am
missing. If you liked them half as much as
you say, you would not make me wait so

long for them. I have thought of them
during all the time of my voyage and think
of them now more than ever. You have
forgotten them.

CXV.

PARIS, *September* 3, 1846.

I HAD imagined that you would prefer one
or two walks with me rather than eight days
of whitebait. But since you are not of the
same opinion, let your will be done! I have
not the courage even not to write to you.
I would not write if I were less foolish. I
am running the risk of finding myself alone
on the blue Rhine. It shall be a little misfortune. But I do not know if I will come
back this way. So we run the risk, I mean
I run the risk, of not meeting till November.
The responsibility rests on you. I know
that it will weigh lightly on you.

CXVI.

METZ, *September* 12, 1846.

I HAVE just arrived here after a sleepless
night in a stage-coach and my head is exces-

sively giddy. It seems to me that my candles are turning on my table. A sail, intermingled with wrecks, is announced for to-morrow, but it does not prevent me from sleeping. I shall probably write to you from some German inn. I learn with a great deal of pleasure that you are lonesome. I predicted this to you.

CXVII.

BONN, *September* 18, 1846.

I HAVE been for six days in this beautiful land of Rhenish Prussia, where civilization is far advanced, except in the matter of beds, which are always four feet long, while the sheets are three feet long. I am leading a German life; that is, rising at five and going to bed at nine, after four meals. Until the present time this mode of life agreed with me well enough and it did not harm me to do anything but open my mouth and my eyes. Only the German women have become horribly homely since my last visit. I have not been pleased by the monuments

I have seen; German architects seem to me to be worse than ours.

CXVIII.

SOISSONS, *October* 10, 1846.

IT seems that you were in very bad humor last Saturday, but you regained your serenity Sunday, although there are small clouds floating over your letter. To continue the metaphor, I would like to see you some day under fixed weather, without previous storms. Unfortunately, it is a habit which you have taken. We separate almost always better friends than when we met. Let us try, therefore, to have, one of these days, the continuous amiability that I have hoped for sometimes. It seems to me that it would be better for us.

When were you at the Italian Opera? Was it Thursday, and were we near each other without knowing it? I should like to have seen you with your court in order to learn if you are in society as I wish you to be. I expect to be in Paris Thursday night, or Friday at the latest. If the weather be fine Saturday, do you wish to go out for a walk ? Good-by, dear friend, I thank you for all the tenderness there is in your letter. I try to forget the harshness that is in it. I like to guess that under it you are all heart and soul; believe that this appears in spite of all your efforts at concealment.

CXIX.

PARIS, *September* 22, 1847.

THE " Revue " troubles me a great deal for " Don Pèdre." I should like to have your opinion on this subject. The work seems to me to have the disadvantage of everything that is done at length and painfully. I have given myself a great deal of trouble for an exactness that none will appreciate.

CXX.

Saturday, February 26, 1848.

I AM becoming accustomed to the strangeness of things and reconciled with the conquerors, who, stranger still, behave like gen-

tlemen. There is now a strong tendency
toward order. If it continues I shall become a republican. The only fault I find
with the new order of things is that I may
not be able to make a living in it and that
I am deprived of seeing you.

CXXI.

PARIS, *March*, 1848.

IF misfortune comes to you, let us try to
console each other. Each day must bring
to us new griefs. We shall give to each
other the share of courage which we retain.
Shall we see each other to-morrow, or after ?
It seems to me that we have not met for a
century. Good-by. You were very amiable the other day and I regret that you
were not amiable for a longer time.

CXXII.

PARIS, *March*, 1848.

I THINK that you are too frightened.
Things are not worse than they were yes-

terday, which does not mean that they are right and that there is no danger. As for your project of travel, it is difficult to give advice. There are people who think that Paris is safer than any provincial town. I am of that opinion. If civil war should begin I think it would be declared in the provinces. There is great irritation in them already against the dictatorship of the capital. I do not believe that there is immediate danger.

CXXIII.

Saturday, March 11, 1848.

I AM anxious about your sore throat. Take care of yourself and try to forget all that is happening. I should like to have something other than your shadow. I regret that you retired so early. The happiness of seeing you is as great under the Republic as under the Monarchy. We must not be too miserly. In what a strange world we are living! But the most important thing to say to you is that I love you every day more and more.

CXXIV.

PARIS, *March* 13, 1848.

I HAD hoped that you would not go out of town so quickly. I wrote to you yesterday, expecting to see you to-day. You do not tell me how long you intend to remain away, drinking milk. I wish you were in Paris with a new bonnet for Thursday's reception at the Academy, where new bonnets are to be rare, I fear. I make this request in the academic interest. In mine, I count on going out walking with you Saturday.

CXXV.

PARIS, *Wednesday, May* 15, 1848.

ALL went well, because the rioters are so foolish that, in spite of all the faults of the Chamber, the latter was stronger than they. There are no killed nor wounded. The National Guard and the people have excellent sentiments. All the chiefs of the mobs have been arrested. I hope we shall meet Saturday. I was present at very dramatic scenes, which I will relate to you.

CXXVI.

June 27, 1848.

I RETURNED home this morning, after a short campaign of four days which was without peril for me, but wherein I saw all the horrors of this time and of this country. I do not know if it will ever be possible to turn off the savagery wherein we fall so often. Do not believe all that the newspapers say of deaths and destructions. The ravage is not as great as people say. These are the most curious things which I saw :

1. The prison was guarded for several hours by the National Guard and surrounded by insurgents. They said to the National Guard, "Do not fire on us and we shall not fire. Keep the prisoners."

2. I went into a house on the corner of the Bastile Square to see the battle. It had just been won by the insurgents. I asked of the residents there, "Did they take much from you ?" They replied, "Nothing was stolen."

Add to this the fact that I took to the

prison a woman who was cutting off the
heads of the soldiers with her kitchen knife
and a man whose arms were red with blood
from having washed them in wounds.

CXXVII.

Paris, *July* 2, 1848.

I HAVE great need of seeing you in order
to make up for the sad scenes of last week.
Paris is, and shall be, quiet for a long time.
I do not think that the social war is at an
end; but a new battle as frightful seems to
me to be impossible. An infinity of circumstances, which may not occur again, led to
it. When you return you shall not find the
hideous traces which your imagination probably represents to you. What Paris lacks
the most is you. I am thinking of you incessantly. I was thinking of you while I
looked at the deserted houses and the
battle.

CXXVIII.

Paris, *July* 9, 1848.

You are like Antæus, who regained
strength as soon as he touched the soil.

You had no sooner reached your native country than you fell again into old defects. I asked you to tell me how long you intended to remain out of town. A figure was not difficult to write. But you prefer to send three pages of circumlocutions wherein I cannot understand anything. I see that you spend your time most agreeably. In brief, I am much displeased by your letter. Good-by. Write to me soon.

CXXIX.

PARIS, *Monday, July* 19, 1848.

YOU divine things perfectly when you take the trouble and you have sent what I asked for; what matters it if it be a repetition? Am I not like the ex-king, Louis Philippe? Like him, " I receive always with renewed pleasure," etc. The truth is that our chances of tranquillity are greatly increased. It required several years of organization for the riots of June 23d to 26th. A second representation of that bloody tragedy seems impossible to me; as long, at least, as actual conditions are not materially changed.

But let us quit politics. You cannot form an idea of the pleasure that you would do me by accepting my invitation to breakfast.

CXXX.

PARIS, *Saturday, August* 5, 1848.

HAVE I translated for you a very pretty ballad of a Greek who returns to his home after a long absence and whom his wife does not recognize ? Like Penelope she asks him for details about his house; he answers correctly, but she is not convinced; she asks for other details, which she obtains, and then she recognizes him. All this is left to your powers of divination. Good-by; I am waiting for news from you.

CXXXI.

PARIS, *August* 12, 1848.

I CANNOT tell you how angry I am with you. Apricots and prunes have gone out of season and I expected the pleasure of eating some with you. I am perfectly sure that if you had really wished to come you would be in Paris already. I am horribly lonesome and I have a great desire to leave the city without waiting for you. All that I can do is to wait until August 25th, at three o'clock—not an hour longer.

CXXXII.

PARIS, *August* 20, 1848.

THE situation is much embroiled. It resembles that of Rome during Catiline's conspiracy. Only there is no Cicero. The citizen Proudhon has a great number of adepts and his sheets are sold by the thousand. All this is very sad. But the capital point is whether you will be here August 25th. If there be a battle it will be won or lost on that day. The leaves are beginning to turn and to fall. I have been ill for several days; that is why I am sad, perhaps. I need not tell you that I should be vexed to die before our breakfast at Saint-Germain. Good-by, write to me quickly. You ought not to tease people as you do.

9

CXXXIII.

Paris, *August* 23, 1848.

IT was not amiable of you not to answer
sooner. I am still ill. I do not eat nor
sleep. However, I have to work, and it is
not in doing nothing that I am yawning. I
cannot understand why you stay away so
long. I can find no other explanation of
your sojourn among the savages than that
you have made some conquest there of which
you are proud. I have a good quarrel in
reserve for you. Shall it be Friday or Monday ? It would not be prudent of you to
delay longer.

CXXXIV.

Paris, *Saturday, November* 5, 1848.

I HAVE been irritated against you, for
I need to see you. I have been, and am
still, very ill and frightfully sad. An hour
with you would cure me. You did not
even take the trouble to write something
amiable to me. I have to forgive you

always, but I wish you would do something
to deserve forgiveness.   Will you do something to make up for my lonesomeness of a
fortnight ?   I leave to your intelligence the
application of adequate damages.

CXXXV.

LONDON, *June* 1, 1850.

I SHALL not tell you much of my impressions.   Decidedly, Englishmen are individu-
ally stupid and collectively admirable.   All
that may be done with money, common
sense and patience they do; but they have
no more idea of the arts than my cat.   We
are going to Hampton Court in order to
avoid the offers of suicide which the Lord's
day makes.   All the women seem to me to
be made of wax.   They wear bustles so
considerable that there is room on the Re-
gent Street sidewalk for only one woman.
I visited yesterday the new House of Commons, which is a frightful monstrosity.   I
never knew before what one could do with
absolute lack of taste and two million pounds
sterling.   I fear to become a socialist by

eating dinners that are too good, in gold
plate. But there is no probability of a revolution here. The poor people are servile
unto strangeness.

CXXXVI.

SALISBURY, *Saturday, June* 15, 1850.

I HAVE enough of this country. I have
an indigestion of perpendicular architecture
and of the perpendicular manners of the
natives. I am particularly furious against
Oxford. One fellow had the insolence to
invite me to dinner. There was a fish of
four inches in a grand silver dish and a lamb
chop in another dish. All this served in
magnificent style, with potatoes in a carved
wood dish. But I was never so hungry.
This is an indication of the hypocrisy of the
people. They like to show to strangers
that they are moderate, and, provided they
lunch, do not dine. I have just made a
bull. I gave a half crown to a gentleman
in black who showed me the cathedral, and
then I asked him to give me the address of
a gentleman to whom the dean had written

a letter of introduction for me. It happened
that the man to whom I gave the half crown
and the man to whom the letter was ad-
dressed were the same person. He looked
silly for a while, and so did I; but he kept
the money. My letter will go, God knows
when! I have just been told that on the
Lord's day the post-office rests. The women
here wear hoops under their gowns. It is
impossible to see anything more ridiculous
than an English woman in a hoop.

CXXXVII.

BASLE, *October* 10, 1850.

HERE I am in a model republican land
where there are neither custom-house officers
nor policemen, and where the beds are of
my size. Good-by; you must be, lazy as
you are, pleased because I write you so late,
since it will excuse you from the task of
replying to me.

CXXXVIII.

PARIS, *Monday, June* 15, 1851.

I WENT out yesterday for the first time
to see the Spanish dancers at Princess Ma-

thilde's. They are mediocre. Moreover,
these ladies wore such a quantity of crinoline in the back and so much cotton in front
that it was evident civilization is invading
everything. I have just received your
cushion. You are really a very skilful work-
man. I would never have suspected it.
Good-by. I do not know how to thank you.

CXXXIX.

LONDON, *Saturday, July* 22, 1851.

I AM sad at your departure. I have not
even the consolation of scolding you. Try
to return by the first days of August. The
Crystal Palace is a great Noah's Ark, marvellous by the singularity of the objects
which one sees there, very mediocre from an
artistic point of view. I am so vexed by
your letter that I have not the courage to
write. Good-by.

CXL.

PARIS, *Thursday night, December* 2, 1851.

IT seems to me that the last battle is being
fought. Who shall win ? If the president

should lose, it seems to me that the heroic deputies will have to yield the place to Ledru-Rollin. The military men say that they are sure of success; but you know what their predictions mean.

CXLI.

PARIS, *December* 3, 1851.

WHAT shall I say ?   I know no more than you do.   It is certain that the soldiers have a ferocious air and frighten the bourgeois this time.   We are navigating toward the unknown.   Tell me when I shall see you.

CXLII.

March 24, 1852.

I HAVE all sorts of trouble, besides a great deal of work.   In fine, I have undertaken a chivalrous work impulsively, and you know that one should guard against impulses.   I repent at times.   The innocence of Libri has been demonstrated to me and I am writing an article for the " Revue " about his suit. Pity me; one gains only hard knocks in such a trade, but injustice revolts one so much at times that it makes one stupid.*

I am sorry to learn of the death of a person whom you liked. It is one reason more for us to meet often. You are right to think that life is a silly thing, but let us not make it worse than it is. After all, there are good moments in it, and the remembrance of these good moments is more agreeable than that of bad ones is sad. We must make an ample provision of good recollections.

CXLIII.

Paris, *April* 22, 1852.

I am threatened with a suit for contempt of court. I should not have attacked the judgment against Libri. I shall have to submit to interrogations. I hope that in the battle I shall have regained my energy. At present, I am annoyed and nervous.

---

* Libri was not innocent. An Italian bibliographer, very learned and seductive in manner, he robbed the National Library of valuable manuscripts, which have been found in private collections in England. Whenever they are offered at public sales the National Library claims them as stolen goods, and gets them.

CXLIV.

Friday night, May 1, 1852.

MY good mother is dead.   I hope she did not suffer too much.   Her features were calm and she wore her usual sweet expression.   I thank you for your interest in her. Good-by; think of me.

CXLV.

PARIS, *May* 19, 1852.

COME quickly; I have a great quantity of things to say to you.   I do not know if they wish to hang me or not.   What makes me fidgety is the thought of a public ceremony before the flower of the rabble and three imbeciles in black gowns, stiff as pickets, and persuaded that they are something. Good-by.

CXLVI.

PARIS, *May* 22, 1852.

WAS our walk tiresome ?   Say no quickly. I was waiting for a word from you.   I have

been confiscated by my lawyer.   He seems
to be a man of wit, not too eloquent.   I
have hopes.

CXLVII.

May, 1852, *Wednesday,* 5 *o'clock.*

FIFTEEN days of imprisonment and one
thousand francs fine! My lawyer spoke very
well; my judges were very polite; I was not
at all nervous.   In fine, I am not as much
displeased as I should be.   I shall not take
an appeal.

CXLVIII.

May 27, 1852, *at night.*

MY revenge has begun already.   My
friend Saulcy was at a house where they
were talking of the judgment against me,
yesterday; when, heedlessly, he said such
big words as silliness, fatuity, stupidity,
conceit of snobs, and so forth, appealing to
a gentleman in evening dress whom he
knew by sight, but whose profession he did
not know.   The gentleman was one of my
judges.   Imagine the state of mind of the
hostess, the guests, and of Saulcy himself,

who fell on a sofa laughing to death and
saying, " Nevertheless, I retract nothing!"

CXLIX.

Monday night, June 1, 1852.

I SPEND all my time reading the letters of
Beyle.   That makes me at least twenty
years younger.   It is like making an au-
topsy of the thoughts of a man whom I knew
intimately and whose ideas of things and
men have singularly affected mine.   That
makes me sad and joyful twenty times an
hour.

CL.

MARSEILLES, *September* 12, 1852.

I NEED your presence in this country
which seems so dull to me.   I would make
you eat twenty different kinds of fruits that
you do not know.   For example, yellow
peaches, white and red melons, and fresh
peanuts.   Moreover, you might spend a
day in Turkish curiosity shops where there
are inutilities the most agreeable to see and
the most disagreeable to pay for.   I have

asked myself often why you do not come to
the south of France, and never find a reason.

CLI.

MOULINS, *September* 27, 1852.

I HAVE had for forty-five hours such a
disposition to congestion of the brain that
I felt as if I were going to the land of the
shades. I was absolutely alone and I treated
myself, or, rather, did not treat myself at all,
for I was in a state of physical and moral
prostration which would have made painful
the least exertion. I felt some annoyance
at the thought of going to an unknown
world; but it was still more annoying to resist. It is through brutal resolution, I think,
that one quits this world; not because illness
triumphs, but because one has become indifferent to everything and makes no defence.

CLII.

CARABANCHEL, *September* 11, 1853.

WHEN I arrived here they were preparing
to celebrate the anniversary of the hostess.

They were to play a comedy in her honor
and in that of her daughter. I had to manu-
facture skies, repair scenes, design costumes
and so forth. Then I had to direct rehear-
sals of five mythological goddesses, only one
of whom had ever played in private theatri-
cals. All went well. This morning I have
a terrible headache. As there are nine ladies
here, without a man, I am called in Madrid,
Apollo. Of the nine muses, there are,
unfortunately, five who are mothers or
aunts of the four others; but these four are
Andalusians with little ferocious airs that
become them ravishingly, especially when
they are wearing the Olympian costume.

CLIII.

THE ESCURIAL, *October* 5, 1853.

I SEND you a little flower which I found
on the mountain behind the ugly convent
of the Escurial. At night, when the wind
passes over it, the odor of it is delightful.
I found the Escurial as sad as when I left it
twenty years ago, but civilization has reached
here. There are iron beds, chops, no bugs
nor monks.

CLIV.

MADRID, *October* 25, 1853.

BULLS have no more heart and men are not worth much more. I think of beginning my archæologic voyage as soon as the weather is settled. It is probable that if you send your orders I shall receive them in time to fill them. Unfortunately, I do not know what to buy in this country. I bought, at all events, handkerchiefs the design of which is very ugly; but it seemed to me that you liked one of those handkerchiefs which came to me I know not from where. Do you want garters and buttons? At Madrid nobody reads. I have asked myself how the women pass the time and found no plausible answer. They are all thinking of becoming empresses. A lady of Granada was at the playhouse when some one announced in her box that the Countess Teba was to marry the French Emperor. She rose impetuously, exclaiming, " In this country there is no future."

Among my diversions I have forgotten to

mention an academy of history, whereof I
am a member.   Good-by.

CLV.

MADRID, *November 22*, 1853.

I SHALL bring you garters, since you do
not want buttons.   I discovered them not
without trouble.   Civilization is making
such rapid progress that elastics have re-
placed on almost all legs the classic ligas of
the past.   When I asked the maids here to
tell me where the shops were, they crossed
themselves in indignation, saying that they
did not wear such old things, which were
good enough only for the common people.
The progress in French fashions is frightful.
Mantillas are rare.   Bonnets replace them.
You should rejoice at the masterpieces of
the dressmakers in this capital.   We had on
the 15th a ball to celebrate Saint Eugenie.
The wife of the United States Minister wore
a costume which made everybody laugh.
Black velvet embroidered with braid and
spangles and a theatrical diadem.   Her son

sent a challenge to a duel to a duke, very
noble, very rich, very dull and anxious to
live long.   Good-by.

CLVI.

MADRID, *November* 28, 1853.

THE house where I live is a neutral ground
where ministers and chiefs of the opposition
meet, which is agreeable for those who want
news.   Wherever one goes in Madrid, provided one goes to a public place, one is sure
of meeting the same three hundred persons.
The result is a very amusing society, infinitely less hypocritical than elsewhere.   I
must tell you a good story.   The custom
here is to offer everything that is praised.
The Prime Minister's sweetheart was dining
the other day beside me; she is as foolish as
a cabbage and very big.   She displayed
beautiful shoulders on which fell a garland
with tassels of metal or glass.   Not knowing what to say to her, I praised both shoulders and garland, and she replied, "At your
disposition."

CLVII.

PARIS, *July* 29, 1854.

MY minister has offered to send me to
Munich as commissioner of I know not
what. I said neither yes nor no. Probably
you intend to spend some time in London.
My last days there were amusing and interesting. I met all the politicians. I was
present at the debate on the budget in the
House of Lords and in the Commons, and
all the celebrated orators spoke, wickedly it
seemed to me. I have brought from London a pair of garters. I do not know what
English women put on their stockings, nor
how they procure this indispensable article,
but I think it must be a very difficult thing
to get and very trying to their virtue. The
clerk who gave me these garters blushed to
his ears. You write amiable things which
would please me greatly if experience had
not made me distrustful. I dare not hope
what I desire most ardently.

10

CLVIII.

PARIS, *August* 2, 1854.

I DO not believe in your impossibilities. I retain my doubts and my grief. My minister wishes me to go to the exhibition at Munich. I have no desire to go. Good-by; I love you whatever you do and I think you should be affected by this.

CLIX.

INNSPRUCK, *August* 31, 1854.

I AM eating delicious snipe and drinking extraordinary soups. The drawback of this voyage is ignorance of the manners and of the ideas of the people. The women in the Tyrol seem to me to be treated as they deserve. They are attached to carts and made to drag heavy loads. They are very homely, with enormous feet. The beautiful ladies whom I met on the railway trains or on boats are not much better looking. They wear indecent bonnets and blue brogans with apple-green gloves.

CLX.

I AM ill and out of sorts. The faces here are very different from those of Germany: big heads, large shoulders, little hips and no legs. This is the description of a Bohemian beauty. I strained my knowledge of anatomy uselessly yesterday to understand how these women walked. They have beautiful eyes and black hair, but feet and hands of a length and of a width which astonish voyagers best accustomed to extraordinary things. I have seen autographs of Ziska and John Huss. They wrote finely though they were heretics.

CLXI.

VIENNA, *October* 2, 1854.

MY guide has presented me to very beautiful ladies. Fashionable society being polite here, they found me amiable. I wrote sublime thoughts in albums. I made drawings; in a word, I was perfectly ridiculous. Did I tell you that I went to Hungary ? My

prudery was shocked at Baden, where men
and women go pell mell in boiling mineral
water.   I saw there a beautiful Hungarian
woman who hid her face with her hands, not
having, like Turkish women, a shirt.   You
would find here magnificent furs for nothing.
Good-by; I am not well pleased with your
last letter.

CLXII.

PARIS, *Sunday, November* 27, 1854.

IT is very unfortunate to lose one's
friends, but it is a calamity which one may
avoid only by a greater calamity, which is
not to like anybody.   Above all, one must
not forget the living for the dead.   You
should have come to see me instead of writing to me.   We might have talked on the
vanities of this world.   I remained all day
by the fireside in misanthropic disposition.

CLXIII.

LONDON, *July* 20, 1856.

I HAVE found here people so amiable that
it is evident they are very lonely.   I met

two of my ancient beauties: one is become
asthmatic and the other a Methodist.   Then
I made the acquaintance of eight or ten
poets who seemed to me to be more ridiculous than ours.

CLXIV.

EDINBURGH, *July* 26, 1856.

I HOPED to get a letter from you.   None
came.   I am going with a Scotchman to see
his castle beyond the lakes.   I spent three
days at the Duke of Hamilton's.   There are
paintings by great masters, Greek and
Chinese vases and magnificent books.   All
these things are arranged without taste, and
it is evident that their owner does not enjoy
them.   I understand now why the Frenchman is liked in foreign lands.   He takes the
trouble to enjoy himself and thus he amuses
others.   The Scottish accent is odious to
me.   The women are very ugly.   I am
shocked by the proportion of reddish hair
that I meet.

CLXV.

Sunday, August 3, 1866.
From a country house near Glasgow.

I SPENT three days at the Marquis of Breadalbane's. There is a herd of American bisons, very ferocious, imprisoned in a peninsula. Bisons and marquis have an air of being bored. I have just heard a story which pleases me. An Englishman walks in front of a hencoop Saturday night and hears a great noise of cocks and hens. He imagines that some fox is in there and warns the keeper. The keeper answers: " Oh, we are only separating the cocks from the hens because to-morrow will be the Lord's day."

CLXVI.

KINLOCH-LINCHARD, *August* 16, 1856.
I AM not pleased with your letter. Think again and then say yes or no.

CLXVII.

CARABANCHEL, *Thursday, December*, 1856.

I TOOK advantage of this beautiful weather to sprain my wrist, and if I am able to write to you the reason is that I was instructed in the American method wherein one does not move the fingers. The sprain came through my horse's fault. He threw me over his head while I was lighting a cigar. I do not sleep better than in Paris, although I go to bed at eleven. There is a Countess Apraxine here who smokes, wears round hats, and has a goat in her drawing-room. But the most amusing person here is Lady Shelley, who wrote yesterday to the French consul: " Lady Shelley announces to the French consul that she will give an English dinner, after which she will be charmed to see him to-day at five minutes after nine o'clock." She wrote to Madame Vigier, " Lady Shelley would be charmed to see Madame Vigier if she would kindly bring her music with her." Madame Vigier replied, " Madame Vigier would be charmed to see Lady Shelley if she would kindly come to her house and behave like a well-bred woman."

CLXVIII.

LAUSANNE, *August* 24, 1857.

IT seems to me that you might have varied your tirades of enthusiasm, on the pleasure of travelling, with some flattering compliments, by way of consolation for those who have not the privilege of accompanying you. I forgive you, however, because of your inexperience with travelling. You say that you will be away for three weeks only. I give you a month. I pray you to consider only that September 28th is an unfortunate anniversary for me, because I was born September 28th. It would be agreeable to me to spend the day in your company.

Good-by; enjoy yourself; do not tire yourself; think of me. I send you a leaf grown six thousand feet above the level of the sea.

CLXIX.

PARIS, *September* 8, 1857.

WHILE you are enthusiastic, I am very ill of a frightful cold. I hope this will move

you.   I do not see why you should stay
three days at Lucerne, unless you spend
your time on the lake.   But it is useless to
give you advice which will reach you too
late.   If you had arranged your affairs with
some strategy we might have met in your
travels.   If I were not so ill that it is impossible for me to assemble two ideas, I would
take advantage of your absence by working.
I am sorry that you do not carry Beyle's
work with you to Italy.   He liked Milan
particularly, because he fell in love there.
I wish I could go into a gondola with you.

CLXX.

AIX, *January* 6, 1858.

FROST, snow, atrocious cold.   I do not
know if I shall be able to go to Burgundy;
however, I shall start for Paris to-morrow
night.   I trust that you will wish me a
happy new year in person.   I met at Nice
all sorts of fine people, among others the
Duchesse de Sagan, who is always young
and ferocious.

CLXXI.

PARIS, *Monday night, January 29,* 1858.

I HAVE not seen you for a century. It is true that many things have happened! I am cured, and attribute this to our last walk. Write to me, I pray you, for I need to see you in order to forget all the horrors of this world.

CLXXII.

LONDON, BRITISH MUSEUM,
Tuesday night, April 28, 1858.

YOU cannot form an idea of the beauty of the British Museum on Sunday, when there is absolutely nobody there except Panizzi and me. It takes then a marvellous attitude of piety; only, one fears that the statues may descend from their pedestals and dance the polka. Good-by, dear friend.

CLXXIII.

LONDON, BRITISH MUSEUM,
May 3, 1858.

I WAS invited to a dinner of the literary fund and warned that I should have to

speak.   I consented, with the pleasure that
you may imagine, and said silly things in
bad English for a quarter of an hour to an
assembly of three hundred men of letters, or
so-called, and one hundred women, admitted
to the honor of seeing us eat tough chicken.
I received yesterday the visit of a lady and
her husband, who wished to sell autograph
letters of Napoleon to Josephine.   They are
interesting letters, for they are full of love.
I do not understand why Josephine did not
burn them immediately after receiving them.

CLXXIV.

PARIS, *May* 19, 1858.

I HAVE been accusing you of taking from
me a book for which I searched as if it were
a needle.   I found it this morning in a corner where I had placed it myself.   I wish I
could talk with you at length before your
departure.   It seems to me that we have
never talked together.

CLXXV.

PALACE OF FONTAINEBLEAU,
May 20, 1858.

I AM half poisoned for having taken too
much laudanum. Besides, I wrote verses
for his Netherlandish Majesty, played in a
comedy and made a fool of myself. What
shall I say of the life which we are leading
here ? We hunted a deer yesterday. We
ate on the grass. Every day we eat too
much. Destiny had not made me a courtier.
I wish I could talk with you in this beautiful
forest.

CLXXVI.

PARIS, *June* 14, 1858.

WHEN a woman has as much taste as you
have, she should not say of a well-written
book that it is immoral. You should say
that the good in the book is good. Do not
judge of things with your prejudices. You
become day by day more prudish. I will
let you wear crinoline, but I will not let you
be prudish. You must know how to look
for the good where it is. I am not in a

humor to say pretty things to you. I am displeased with you, but I shall have to forgive you, of course.

CLXXVII.

INTERLAKEN, *July* 3, 1858.

I FELL in a hole with my horse, but we got out of it without other inconvenience than extreme coolness for an hour or two. A Yankee lady whom we met made, at the same place, a picturesque somersault.

CLXXVIII.

INNSPRUCK, *July* 25, 1858.

SALZBURG seems to me to deserve its German reputation. Happily, it is an unknown land for most tourists. There are no Englishmen there to bore you with their faces. The most beautiful women of the Tyrol are in the Zitterthal, they say. I saw many pretty women there, but too well fed. Their legs, which they show to the garter—it is not as high as you might think—are dazzlingly big.

CLXXIX.

VENICE, *August* 15, 1858.

YOU were making improper comparisons of Mont Blanc with Sugarloaf while I was exterminating myself searching for shells for you. I never saw anything uglier. It is probable that the custom houses that I have to traverse will break them into little pieces, or seize them entire. I rejoice at this in advance, for such a commission was never before given to a man of taste. Venice has filled me with sadness. The architecture is effective, but tasteless and without imagination. I am filled with indignation against the commonplaces that have been written about it. The streets are full of charming girls, bare-footed and bare-headed, who, if they were bathed and scrubbed, would be Venuses.

CLXXX.

GENOA, *September* 10, 1858.

THE lake of Como pleased me. I stopped at Bellaggio. I found in a pretty villa by the lakeside, Madame Pasta, whom I had not

seen since the time when she was triumphant
in Italian opera.   She has increased singularly in width.   She cultivates her cabbages
and says that she is as happy as when we
threw crowns and sonnets at her.   I shall
expect you in Paris October 1st.

CLXXXI.

CANNES, *October* 8, 1858.

YOUR shells have arrived here intact.   I
shall be in Paris Wednesday or Thursday.
If you want your shells come and get them.
Florence is a beautiful city.   Venice is only
pretty.   I find here a complete desert.   All
the hotels are empty and there is not an
Englishman in the streets.   The weather is
superb.   What are your intentions for this
fall ?   One never knows what you will do.
You look one way and row another.   Good-
by.

CLXXXII.

PARIS, *October* 21, 1858.

HERE I am in Paris, furious not to find
you.   Pity me; I bought in Venice a chan-

delier which arrived broken yesterday.   I am
like a stranger here and do not know what
to do with my time.   It would be different
if you were here.

CLXXXIII.

I AM going to Compiègne to-morrow for
four days.   Sandeau came to see me this
morning in all the excitement of a man who
has put on knickerbockers for the first time.
He propounded a hundred questions so naïve
as to alarm me.

CLXXXIV.

MOST of the invited guests left yesterday
and there remained thirty or forty at table.
We took a long walk in the woods.   If it
were not for the cold the forest would be
as beautiful as at the beginning of the fall.
To-day a new cargo of illustrious guests is
expected.   All the Ministers ; then Russians

and other foreigners.   When I think that I might have seen you in Paris to-day I am tempted to abandon everything.

CLXXXV.

THE devil is in our way decidedly.   I have to stay here until December 2d or 3d. I feel like hanging myself when I see you so resigned.

CLXXXVI.

I CONTINUE to rely upon you for the books to be sent to the Lagrenee girls. Think of the responsibility which you have accepted.   You have always been worthy of my confidence.   Your choice of books for young girls has always been exquisite.   If you are going to Florence next year let me know.   It is my greatest desire to be there with you.

CLXXXVII.

CANNES, *January* 7, 1859.

THERE is a great number of Englishmen here.   I dined day before yesterday at Lord Brougham's with I know not how many misses, freshly arrived from Scotland, to whom the sight of the sun seemed to cause great surprise.   If I had the talent to describe costumes I would amuse you with theirs.   Good-by, dear friend, I wish I could send you some of my sunlight.   Take care of yourself and think of me.

CLXXXVIII.

CANNES, *January* 22, 1859.

A MARVELLOUS moonlight, not a cloud, the sea as polished as a mirror, no wind.   I am convinced that the light does me more good than the heat.   We had a day of rain and I felt horrible spasms.   As soon as the sun returned, Richard was himself again.

CXXXIX.

CANNES, *February* 5, 1859.

My windows open on the sea and I can
see the islands from my bed. It is delicious.
The almond trees are in bloom, but the winter was so cold and the summer was so dry
that the jessamines are blighted. I am beginning to count the days. I hope that the
month will not come to an end without my
meeting you.

CXC.

PARIS, *March* 24, 1859.

WERE you at liberty to-day? I supposed
I was engaged for the entire day. This prevented me from writing to you and asking
you to see me. At the last moment I found
myself a free man. I am glad that my
article on Prescott's " Philip II." pleased
you. I am not very well pleased with it,
because I said only half of what I wished
to say. The work is really mediocre. It

seems to me that, if the author had been less a Yankee, he might have done something better.

CXCI.

SOMEBODY gave me a novel by Lady Georgiana Fullerton, written in French, with a request to note the passages that are defective. There is nothing in this book except peasants of the Béarn who eat sandwiches and poached eggs, and ask thirty francs for a basket of peaches. I might as well try to write a Chinese tale. You ought to take this book and correct it for me, in return for all the books which I have lent you that you have never returned.

CXCII.

THERE is in our army a gayety which the Austrians lack absolutely. Although I am not an optimist, I am confident of our success. Our old reputation is so well established that those who fight against us do it with faint hearts. Do not fear; very few bullets hit their mark and the war will not hurt your brother. Be sure that the beautiful Italian ladies will treat our soldiers well. If I were of your brother's age, a campaign in Italy would be to me a most agreeable manner of seeing the awakening of an oppressed people. It is one of the most beautiful spectacles.

CXCIII.

PARIS, *May* 7, 1859.

ALL bullets do not hit their mark and there is a great deal of space above and around a man. Your brother will have made the finest campaign since the Revolution. Among your tribulations are you thinking of an oasis? You and I need it greatly. Nothing would be easier for you, if you wished to do a good act. I can take you here or elsewhere for a week. I shall await your decision impatiently. Good-by, dear friend; be brave. I kiss you very tenderly, as I love you.

CXCIV.

PARIS, *May* 19, 1859.

THE misfortune which may come may not be overcome. It is wise to think of it as little as possible. That is why I desire so much to go with you far from the war, thinking of nothing but leaves and flowers and other agreeable things. If you have read Boccaccio, you know that all great misfortunes come to such an end. Why not let them begin thus ? I have dined at a Chinaman's who gave me an opium pipe. I was suffering from suffocation before I began to smoke; at the third puff I was cured. A Russian who tried the opium after me was completely changed in less than ten minutes: he was very homely; he became truly handsome. This lasted a quarter of an hour.

CXCV.

PARIS, *May* 28, 1859.

YOU have a way of announcing bad news which enrages me. You say always what you would have done, if——! It is like Roland's horse who had all the good qualities, but who is dead. If he had not been dead he would have run faster than the wind. I do not like that style of pleasantry, because it makes your good-will suspicious to me, and because I am vexed at your being so far from me. Your return will be soon, probably. Meanwhile, keep me informed of your acts and projects, for it seems impossible that you shall not do all sorts of wild things. Good-by. Write to me very reasonably, without diplomacy.

CXCVI.

PARIS, *June* 11, 1859.

IF we have all Europe against us, how shall we get out of it without recourse to revolution everywhere ? It seems that Austria intends to send its last soldier to Italy. This is not reassuring, but it is one reason the more to gather strength and courage against the misfortunes which may happen. I am thinking of the weather and the green leaves.

Good-by.   You know that I am waiting impatiently for your letters.   Do not forget to be precise and clear.

CXCVII.

PARIS, *July* 3, 1859.

I AM dying of desire to see you.   My poor devil of a servant received a bullet in the leg at the battle of Solferino.   Everybody in my house is in tears.   I am suffering a great deal and sleep not at all.   Good-by.

CXCVIII.

PARIS, *Tuesday night, July* 20, 1859.

WHEN I make a proposition to you, I do it very seriously always.   All depends on you.   I am invited to go to Scotland and to England.   If you return to Paris I shall not budge.   I shall feel under an extraordinary obligation to you, and if you had an idea of the pleasure that you would do me I am sure that you would not hesitate.

This morning a man dressed in black and having a noble face came to see me.   He

said that God inspired him.   He had been
accused of trying to kill his porter with a
dagger, but it was a crucifix.   While the
man talked he kept his hand in the pocket of
his coat, and I expected him to draw from it
a dagger.   He could find one easily on my
table.   There was nothing near me except
a Turkish pipe, and I was calculating the
moment when prudence would dictate that I
should break it on his head.   At last he drew
from his terrible pocket a rosary.   He fell
on his knees.   I retained a glacial coolness,
but I was afraid, for what can one do with a
madman ?

CXCIX.

Paris, July 21, 1859.

My letter of yesterday crossed yours.
Yours was not a letter, but a curling-paper.
I am reading the " Letters of Madame du
Deffand," which will amuse you.   They impress me with the sincerity and the fidelity
of the writer's affections.   These people
were more amiable than we and than you,
whom I love no more.   Good-by.   I am in
too bad a humor to write more.

CC.

I SHALL be in Paris until August 15th, after which I shall probably go to the Highlands, but it is well understood that you shall have the preference over everything, and you may expect me any day that you will appoint. You see that I am precise. It seems that you cannot live without mountains and old forests. I should be charmed to see you. I sometimes suspect that I am travelling on the grand railway which goes beyond the tomb. At times the idea is painful; at others, I find in it the consolation which one feels in railway trains: the absence of responsibility before a force superior and irresistible.

CCI.

I SHALL call on you before the end of the month. When you want to delay negotiations, you are more skilful in finding dilatory

means than the Austrian diplomats. It is
well understood that I shall accept good reasons, reasonable objections; but they must
be made with frankness. You know very
well that whenever I shall have to choose
between the greatest happiness for me and
the least inconvenience for you I shall not
hesitate. Good-by.

CCII.

PARIS, *Saturday, September* 3, 1859.

I FEAR that we shall not meet again this
year and I do not wish to go without saying
good-by to you. I shall start Monday for
Tarbes, where I shall remain probably until
the 12th or 15th. I shall return to Paris for
a few days and then go to Spain. If I believed in presentiments I would not go beyond the Pyrenees, but I must make my
visit, which shall be the last probably, to
Madrid. Without being ill, I am so nervous
that it is worse than an illness. I am consoled by the thought that you are enjoying
yourself. Take care of yourself, eat and
sleep, since you can.

CCIII.

PARIS, *September* 15, 1859.

MY trip to the Pyrenees has done me good. Their Majesties were in good health at Saint-Sauveur. I have admired the natives, who had the good taste not to follow them wherever they went. The Emperor bought there a dog of the ancient Pyrenean race. It is a little larger than a donkey.

CCIV.

PARIS, *September* 20, 1859.

ALTHOUGH you have made me furious this summer with your ifs and your noes, I assure you that it saddens me not to say good-by to you. Who knows if you will be in Paris when I return ? I am going in a dark mood. I hope that your ideas are rose-colored. I shall regret Paris because I might have seen you there. You are its only attraction for me.

CCV.

MADRID, *October* 21, 1859.

I RECEIVED with great happiness your little letter and your amiable souvenir. I arrived here wearied by all sorts of little troubles. Your letter, which had preceded me in Madrid through excess of zeal of one of my friends, was lost for several days and could not be found easily. The ladies whom I had left thin have become elephants, for the climate of Madrid is fattening. Expect to see me increased by a third. Yet I hardly eat and I am not well. At night I go to the opera, which is pitiful. I went Monday to a bull-fight, which was not amusing. The bulls have become oxen, and the spectacle resembles too much an abattoir.

CCVI.

CANNES, *January* 2, 1860.

I WISH you a happy new year. Here is a good story of this country. A farmer near

Grasse was found dead in a ravine, where he had fallen or had been thrown at night. Another farmer came to see one of my friends and told him that he had killed the man. "How and why did you do it?" The man answered, "He had cursed my sheep. Then I went to my shepherd, who gave me three needles that I put to boil in a pot, and I said over the pot words which he taught me. The same night that I put the pot, on the fire the man died." Do not be astonished that my books were burned at Grasse on the square in front of the church. I am going there Tuesday for a few days. I am promised monuments of all sorts and beautiful mountains.

CCVII.

CANNES, *January* 22, 1860.

I HAVE seen beautiful rocks, cascades, and precipices. I have spent a week in admiration of pure nature. I have contracted from it horrible pains and I have been in bed for two days.

CCVIII.

CANNES, *February* 4, 1860.

WHEN is your fête day ? It seems to me
that your name is Lutheran or heretical. Is
your patron saint the Evangelist or the Bap-
tist ? When is his fête day ? You guess that
I wish to surprise you. I am waiting for
two of my friends, who are to spend a week
with me. Good-by; I shall see you next
month. Meanwhile, I am ill, melancholy,
bored. I am losing my eyesight, and could
not draw even if my health permitted it.
How sad it is to grow old! Good-by.

CCIX.

CANNES, *February* 21, 1860.

I RECEIVED only the day before yesterday
a letter from my cousin about the Byzantine
buckle. I send you her textual opinion.
She says that this buckle is charming, too
charming for her and a great deal too young.
However, to correct her severe judgment,
she adds that she has just ordered a gown

to fit the buckle. If you are not satisfied
with your success you are hard to please.
Good-by, take care of yourself. Do not go
out at night.

CCX.

Paris, *Sunday night, March* 12, 1860.

While I was at Cannes I read a novel by
Bulwer—"What Will He Do With It?"
—which seemed to me to be senile to the
last degree. The hero and heroine surpass
all that usage makes permissible in the stupid
style. I learned to-day that at one of the
most recent masked balls a woman had the
courage to wear the costume of 1806 without a crinoline, and made a sensation.

CCXI.

Paris, *April* 4, 1860.

I need you to take life patiently. It becomes day by day more and more a bore.
People are so stupid. I have bought several beautiful books. Have you read the
" Memoirs of Holland," attributed to Ma-

dame de Lafayette ?   I will lend them to
you when you come, provided you give me
good security.   The volumes are bound by
Bauzonnet.

CCXII.

Saturday, April 13, 1860.

I HAVE been leading a dissipated life since
Easter.   I went to two balls and dined out
every day.   One ball which I was to attend
is postponed because the accomplices of
Ortega, among whom are two relatives of
the Empress, are on trial in Spain.

CCXIII.

Tuesday night, May 1, 1860.

THE ball at the Alba's was splendid.   The
costumes were beautiful.   The gowns were
outrageously short at the top and at the bottom also.   I saw a great number of charming feet and many garters in the waltz.   The
crinoline is in its decadence.   Believe me, in
two years gowns shall be short, and women
who have natural advantages will distinguish
themselves from those who have only arti-

12

ficial ones. The daughter of a lord was
dressed as a dryad in a gown which would
have revealed her entire bust if she had not
thought of wearing fleshings under it. The
ballet of the elements was composed of sixteen women, all pretty, in short skirts and
covered with diamonds. The naiads were
powdered with silver, which fell on their
shoulders like drops of water. The Salaman-
ders were powdered with gold. The dining-
room, the servants in costumes of pages of
the sixteenth century, all illuminated by
electric light, made one think of Belshazzar's
feast. The Emperor changed his domino
every few minutes and never failed to be
recognized. The Empress wore a white
burnous and a black silk mask which disguised her not at all.

CCXIV.

Saturday, May 12, 1860.

You shall probably be astonished to learn
that I work and write as in my fine days.
When we meet, I will tell you through what
singular circumstance I have shaken my

antique laziness. It would be too long to write. Good-by. I think of you incessantly, despite all your faults.

CCXV.

PALACE OF FONTAINEBLEAU,
June 12, 1860.

I SHALL not think for an instant of your not waiting for me. It would be absurd of you to go to the seashore this warm weather. Tell your friends to be patient. I have to be patient and tell a hundred times the same thing to a person who will not listen.

CCXVI.

PARIS, *Sunday night, July* 2, 1860.

I DO not want to refer again to your expedition. Many things may happen to change your projects. You know mine. I shall remain at the British Museum till the end of July; then go to Bath and to Scotland, where I shall await till September an invitation from you. Good-by.

CCXVII.

PARIS, *Thursday, July* 12, 1860.

I HAVE just finished a long report on the Library of Paris. I lose my time in meddling with what does not concern me. I sometimes desire to write a novel, but whenever I begin one some silly administrative things are given to me to arrange.

CCXVIII.

LONDON, BRITISH MUSEUM,
July 20, 1860.

IT is very amiable of you, assuredly, not to have sent me a word of farewell before my departure. I shall not forgive you till we meet. It takes me some time to become accustomed, in London, to the singular light of the town. It passes, apparently, through brown gauze. I would return to-morrow if you were in Paris. Good-by; I am not pleased with you.

CCXIX.

9 SOUTH PARADE, BATH,
Wednesday night, August 8, 1860.

I BOUGHT a blue veil for you before quitting London.   When they are in evening dress and have white cravats, all Englishmen resemble one another.   I advise you to write to me quickly, for I am very sad and need consolation.   This city is very pretty. It is not too full of smoke and it is surrounded by hills covered with grass and trees.   The baths do me good.   Good-by.

CCXX.

LONDON, 18 ARLINGTON ST.,
August 9, 1860.

I AM preoccupied by nothing but the thought of meeting you.   Try to do something on your part in order to gain time. I do not despair of spending several hours with you, if we set our energies together. The more I think of your expedition to Algiers, the more it seems crazy to me.

Everything will be on fire in the Orient this winter. Good-by, dear friend. I am very sad and wish I were angry. I have not the strength to be angry, for I do not scold you.

CCXXI.

GLENQUOICH, *August 22*, 1860.

THE worst things here are little insects called midges. They like my blood and devour my face and hands. I am here with two young women, one a blonde and the other Titian red, both with satin skins, and the horrible midges prefer to attack me. Our principal amusement is fishing. The advantage of it is that the midges fear water. There are fourteen persons here. During the day each one goes his own way. At night, after dinner, each one takes a book or writes letters. To talk, to try to please one another, are things unknown to the English. I am certain that you will do your best to meet me before your voyage. I have had the courage not to wear your blue veil, despite the midges, in order that you should get it fresh.

CCXXII.

PARIS, *September* 14, 1860.

I SHALL have many errands for you at
Algiers. I recommend you to find for me
a characteristic dressing-gown. I wish you
would get acquainted with the women and
tell me frankly what they said to you.

CCXXIII.

September 17, 1860.

YOU complain of not receiving letters
from me and I cannot understand this. It
is a mystery. Let me know what you
think of it. Good-by; take good care of
yourself.

CCXXIV.

PARIS, *October* 7, 1860.

I CAN understand the interest which a
first view of Oriental life has for you. You
say justly that you find at every step some
things that are grotesque and others that are
admirable. There is, in fact, something

grotesque always in the Orientals, as in certain pompous animals at the Zoo. I thank
you for your descriptions, only they are in-
complete. You have had the rare privilege
of seeing Musselman women and you do not
tell me what I should like to know. Do
they make in Algeria, as in Turkey, an exhibition of their charms ? I should like to
know the characteristics of the dancers whom
you saw—if they were modest; and if they
were not, why not.

CCXXV.

Paris, *October* 16, 1860.

You have promised me an exact description of a quantity of things that I cannot
see. Thanks to the privileges of your sex,
you can go into harems and talk with the
women. I would like to know how they are
dressed, what they do, what they say, what
they think of you. I suppose the dances
are more interesting than those of Paris,
but I want detailed descriptions of them.
Have you understood the sense of what you
have seen ? You know that everything

which regards the history of humanity is full
of interest to me. Good-by, dear friend.
Write to me often; tell me what you are
doing. Many details.

CCXXVI.

PARIS, *October* 24, 1860.

I THANK you for the descriptions you
sent me, although they need illustrations
and a perpetual commentary, especially with
regard to the dances of the natives. From
what you say I imagine they are like the
dances of the gitanas in Granada. Probably
the intention is the same. I am sure that
an Arab of the Sahara who saw a waltz in
Paris would take it for a pantomime. When
one goes to the bottom of things one arrives
always at original ideas. You have noticed
this when you studied mythology with me.
I cannot admit the timidity of your explanations. There are enough euphemisms at
your disposition to tell me everything, and
you are reticent only to make me pray you
not to be. Give me details of manners and
have no fear of scandalizing me.

CCXXVII.

November 1, at night, 1860.

YOU have given me only sketches of Algerian manners, and I want precise details. There is nothing which you cannot say and you are celebrated for your use of euphemisms. You know how to tell things in an academic way. I want to know all that you have learned. I am preparing for French conquests in China by reading a new novel which Stanislas Julien, the patented Chinaman of our government, has translated. It is the story of two young ladies who are very witty and who write verses about everything. They meet two students who write with the same facility, and engage in an endless combat with quatrains. In these quatrains there is nothing but white dragonflies and blue lotus. It is impossible to find anything more destitute of passion. Evidently, the people who find pleasure in that style of literature are abominable pedants who deserve to be conquered by us. I dined to-day at Prince Napoleon's. Princess

Clothilde admired my cuff-buttons and
asked for the jeweller's address. I said:
" Rue d'Alger, No. 10." Is that right ?
Good-by, dear friend.

CCXXVIII.

MARSEILLES, *November* 17, 1860.

I HAVE only the time to say good morning to you.   Good-by.

MARSEILLES, *November* 18, 1860.

UNFORTUNATELY, it was too late.   The
posters say that the ships leave at four, and
they leave at noon.   Did you go to the
Moorish baths ?   What sort of women did
you meet there ?   I imagine that the habit
of sitting with their legs crossed makes their
knees horrible.   If you do not approve their
fashion in dress I suppose that you will
adopt their *kohl* for the eyes.   Besides being
very pretty, it is excellent as a preservative
from ophthalmia.   You have my authority to
use it.   Do you eat bananas in Algiers ?   It
is the best fruit in the world, in my opinion,
but I should like to eat it with you.   On this
idea, dear friend, I wish you good-night.

CCXXIX.

CANNES, *December* 13, 1860.

YOU write with Lacedemonian concision, and, moreover, use a paper manufactured, doubtless, for you only. Yet you have many interesting things to tell me. You are living among barbarians, where there are many things to observe, and you can observe better than anybody because you are a woman. In spite of this, you have taught me only one thing, which I suspected, and you have not told me what you thought of it. You are not doing your work of a traveller well.

CCXXX.

CANNES, *December* 28, 1860.

I THANK you for the pretty purse which you have sent me. I say purse, but I do not know what it is. But it is very pretty, and the gold embroidery in various colors is exquisite in taste. Only barbarians can do such things. I thank you for the dates and the bananas. If I were in Paris you might send them, but you cannot imagine the negligence of transportation here. When you come, bring them and we will eat them together. I see that Mr. Cobden has visited you. He is a very interesting man, the contrary of an Englishman, because he never says a commonplace and has not many prejudices. Good-by; take care of yourself and enjoy your sun.

CCXXXI.

NICE, *January* 20, 1861.

IF you find some pretty silk stuff which may be washed and has not the air of a woman's gown, make of it a dressing-gown for me, as long as possible, buttoned on the left side in the Oriental fashion.

CCXXXII.

CANNES, *February* 16, 1861.

YOUR absence from Paris has been the cause of two misfortunes. The first is, I forgot the books of the Lagrenee girls; the second is, I forgot Saint Eulalie. There is nothing here which I might send to Paris except flowers, and God knows in what con dition they would reach there. I ask for your advice. I am as troubled as usual, and this time have not the resource to transmit my trouble to you. Good-by, dear friend; take care of yourself.

CCXXXIII.

Paris, *March* 21, 1861.

I DELIVERED my speech in the Senate. I was frightened to death, but I overcame this feeling by saying to myself that I was in the presence of two hundred fools and should not be affected by them. The most bothersome thing in politics is Catholicism. You cannot imagine the degree of exasperation that the Catholics have reached. For nothing at all they jump at you. For example, if you do not show all the whites of your eyes while talking of the saintly martyrs, and if you ask innocently, as I have done, " Who has been martyred ? "

A colossal bore was " Tannhäuser." Some

say that the performance at Paris was in com-
pliance with one of the secret clauses of the
Treaty of Villafranca; others that Wagner
was sent to us in order to force us to admire
Berlioz.   The fact is that it is prodigious.
It seems to me that I might write something
like it to-morrow, inspired by my cat walking on my piano.   The performance was
very furious.   Princess Metternich gave herself a great deal of trouble to make people
think that she understood and to provoke
plaudits which never came.   Everybody
yawned; but everybody wanted to seem to
understand this unanswerable enigma.   I
imagine that your Arabic music prepares one
well for this infernal noise.   The fiasco was
enormous!   Auber said that it was Berlioz
without melody.

CCXXXIV.

PARIS, *April* 2, 1861.

DEAR friend, I am very glad to learn that
you are on this side of the sea.   I have
an agreeable remedy for my pains in the
stomach.   It consists of little pills which

are transparent and which contain liquid
ether. You swallow them, and, a second
after, they break and let the ether escape.
The result is an odd, agreeable sensation. I
recommend them to you as an anodyne, if
you need it.

I do not know if there are as many good
Catholics where you are as in Paris. Our
drawing-rooms have become uninhabitable.
Not only those who were devout, but all the
ex-Voltairians of the political opposition
have become papists. I have no other consolation than that some of them feel obliged
to go to the mass, which must bother them
passably. My former professor, M. Cousin,
who formerly called the pope Bishop of
Rome, has been converted and never misses
a mass. People say that M. Thiers is becoming devout, but it is hard for me to believe
that, because I have always liked him.

I can understand that you may not be able
to tell me now when you intend to return to
Paris, but let me know as soon as you can.
Tell me, dear friend, how you are.

CCXXXV.

PARIS, *Wednesday*, *April* 24, 1861.

I AM writing a history of a Cossack of
the seventeenth century, who was killed in
Moscow with horrible tortures, after he had
hanged and drowned a great number of Boy-
ards.   Good-by, dear friend.

CCXXXVI.

PARIS, SENATE, *May* 15, 1861.

I AM the prey, at the present moment, of
herrings, which the seals of Boulogne have
excited to torment us.   This means that
we are disputing about herrings in this es-
tablishment.   We are threatened with daily
sessions.   I work every night and have the
happiness of having reached the tortures
inflicted upon my hero.   You see, I am near
the end.   The work is long, not very amusing, and very horrible.   I will let you read
it when it is printed.   Is it true that the
herring fishermen of Boulogne are thieves,
who have bought herrings taken by the English and pretend having caught them them-

13

selves ?   Is it true that the herrings have
been seduced by the English and never pass
near our coast ?

CCXXXVII.

PALACE OF FONTAINEBLEAU,
Thursday, June 13, 1861.

I NEVER saw people so wild nor so sense-
less as all magistrates.   I say to myself for
my consolation that if, in twenty years from
now, some antiquarian looks at the " Official
Gazette " of this week he will say that there
was, in 1861, a philosopher full of modera-
tion and of calmness, in an assembly of
young fools.   This philosopher is myself.
I say this without vanity.   In this country,
where magistrates are recruited among men
too stupid to earn a living as lawyers, magistrates are badly paid, but receive the privilege of being insolent and vexing.

The weather is magnificent and the air
of the woods is delicious.   The masters of
the house are, as usual, extremely good and
amiable.   The Princess Metternich is here.
She is vivacious in the German fashion; that

is, she has made for herself a style of origi-
nality formed of two parts of a fast woman
and one of a lady. I fear that she has not
wit enough to sustain the rôle. Good-by,
dear friend.

CCXXXVIII.

PALACE OF FONTAINEBLEAU,
Monday, June 24, 1861.

DEAR friend, I have not budged from
here, and will remain until the end of the
month. I told you that I had a sunstroke.
I am better now, but suffering from lumbago, which I caught from rowing on the
lake. I am waiting for news from you impatiently, but fear the fault is mine. I
promised that I would write you if I quitted
Fontainebleau, but what will you have?
One does nothing here and yet one is never
free. Most of the time is spent waiting.
The great philosophy of the land is to know
how to wait, and it is hard for me to get
trained to it. Our great expectation at this
moment is that of the ambassadors from
Siam, who will arrive Thursday. It is said
that they will present themselves on all

fours, crawling on their knees and elbows.
Some say that they lick the carpet, powdered with candy in view of that operation.
The ladies imagine they are to receive marvellous gifts.   I believe that they are bring-
ing nothing at all and hope to carry away
many beautiful things.   I went to Alise last
Wednesday with the Emperor, who has become a perfect archæologist.   He spent
three hours and a half on the mountain
under a terrible sun, examining vestiges of
the sieges of Cæsar and reading the commen-
taries.   We lost there the skin of our ears
and came back looking like chimney sweep-
ers.   We spent our evenings on the lake or
under the trees, looking at the moon and
hoping for the rain.   Good-by, dear friend;
take care of yourself.   Do not expose yourself to the sun, and give me news of yourself.

CCXXXIX.

PALACE OF FONTAINEBLEAU,
June 29, 1861.

DEAR friend, I received the cigar case,
which is charming, even in comparison with

the gifts of the Siamese ambassadors. My
life here is so preoccupied by nothing that I
have not the time to write. At last, we are
all returning to Paris to-night. We had,
Tuesday, a passable ceremony, quite similar
to that of the "Bourgeois Gentilhomme."
It was the oddest spectacle in the world,
that of a score of black men, quite similar to
monkeys, dressed in gold brocade and wearing white stockings with patent leather shoes,
the sword at the side, all crawling on their
knees and elbows along the Henri II. gallery, carrying their noses on the backs of
those who preceded them. The first ambassador had the hardest work. He wore a
felt hat embroidered with gold which danced
on his head at every movement, and he held
in his hands a gold bowl containing two
boxes, wherein were letters of their Siamese
Majesties. The letters were in silk purses
embroidered with gold. After they had
given the letters and tried to turn back, there
was confusion in the embassy. There were
backs striking faces, sabres entering into
eyes. The aspect was that of a troop of
bugs on a carpet. The Minister of Foreign

Affairs had invented this beautiful ceremony
and exacted that the ambassador should
crawl. People think the Asiatics are more
naïve than they are. I am sure that they
would have been glad if they had been permitted to walk. All the effect of the crawling was lost, because the Emperor lost
patience, made the bugs rise, and spoke English to them. The Empress kissed the little
monkey which they had brought with them
and which they say is the son of one of the
ambassadors. He ran on all fours like a
little rat, and had an intelligent air. The
temporal King of Siam sent his portrait to
the Emperor, and that of his wife, who is
horribly ugly. But you would have been
charmed by the variety and beauty of the
stuffs which they brought. They are gold
and silver, woven so lightly that all is transparent and similar to the light clouds of a
beautiful sunset. They gave to the Emperor
trousers embroidered with enamel, gold, red
and green, and a waistcoat of supple gold
brocade, the designs of which, gold on gold,
are marvellous. The buttons are of gold
with small diamonds and emeralds. I never

saw anything so pretty and splendid. What is singular in the taste of these savages is that there is nothing loud in their stuffs, although they use only dazzling silks, silver and gold. All this is marvellously combined and produces a quiet, harmonious effect. Good-by, dear friend; I expect to go to London, about July 8th or 10th.

CCXL.

LONDON, BRITISH MUSEUM,
July 16, 1861.

I SEE by your last letter, dear friend, that you are as busy as a commander-in-chief the day before a battle. I read in " Tristram Shandy " that, in a house where a woman is with child, all the women assume the right to ill-treat men; that is why I have not written to you sooner. I feared that you might look down on me from the height of your grandeur. I hope that your sister is well and that you are no more anxious. Still, I should be pleased if you advised me officially. This does not mean that you need to send me a printed circular. You know, or do not

know, that there is a new chancellor, who is
old, but whose morals are not. A lawyer
named Stevens sent his clerk with a card to
the chancellor. The clerk is told that my
lord has no house in London, but that he
comes often from the country to a house on
Oxford Terrace. The clerk goes there and
asks for my lord. " He is not here." " Do
you think he will return for dinner ? " " No,
but to sleep, certainly. He sleeps here
every Monday." The clerk leaves the letter, and Stevens is astonished because the
chancellor makes faces at him. The truth
is that my lord has in that house a clandes-
tine acquaintance.

I have been in London since Thursday
and have not had a moment of rest. I run
from morning until night. I am invited to
dinner every day and to concerts and balls
in the evening. I went yesterday to a con-
cert at the Marquis of Lansdowne's. There
was not one pretty woman present, which is
remarkable ; but all of them were dressed as
if the greatest dressmaker had made their
gowns. I never saw such hair-dress. One
old woman wore a crown of diamonds

formed of small stars with a big sun in front, exactly like wax figures at a fair.

CCXLI.

LONDON, BRITISH MUSEUM,
July 25, 1861.

I AM spending my time here in a very monotonous fashion, although I dine out every day and see people and things I have not seen before. I dined at Greenwich yesterday, with great personages who tried to make themselves jolly, not, like the Germans, by throwing themselves out of the window, but by making a great deal of noise. The dinner was abominably long, but the whitebait was excellent. We have unpacked here, twenty-three boxes of antiquities. There are two statues and several very remarkable busts of a good epoch and thoroughly Greek. I went to the House of Commons the other evening and listened to the debate on Sardinia. It is impossible to be more verbose than most of the orators. Gladstone pleased me. I expect to be in

Paris August 8th or 10th. I hope to find
you quietly in some solitude.

CCXLII.

PARIS, *August* 21, 1861.

DEAR friend, I have arrived at last, not
in too good a state of preservation. I do
not know if it is because I ate too much
turtle soup, or because I ran too much in
the sun, but I have again those pains in the
stomach which had left me for a time. They
come in the morning at five o'clock and last
for an hour and a half. I suppose that when
one is hanged one suffers in that way. Our
Imperial Commission for the Universal Exposition is at work. We are making prose
to persuade people who have pictures to
lend them to us, in order that we may send
them to London. It is a passably indiscreet
proposition, and most collectors are Carlists
or Orleanists, who think it is a pious thing
to refuse. I fear we shall not make a good
appearance in London next year. We shall
exhibit only the works done in the last ten
years, while the English will exhibit the

products of their school since 1762. There
is nobody in Paris, which pleases me enough.
I spent six weeks dining out, and it is agreeable now not to be compelled to put on a
white cravat to go to table.   I have no
projects for this fall, but if Madame de
Montijo goes to Biarritz I will call on her
and spend a few days with her.   It seems
to me that you are taking pleasure in the
great number of children your sister has.   I
cannot understand this.   I suppose you let
her put them all on your back, in accordance
with your habit of submitting to oppression
which does not come from me.   Good-by,
dear friend.

CCXLIII.

PARIS, *August* 31, 1861.

DEAR friend, I have received your letter,
which seems to announce that you are hap-
pier than you have been for a long time.   I
rejoice at it.   There is little disposition in
me to love children; still, I can understand
attachment for a little girl, as for a little cat,
an animal which your kind resembles much.
I am always ill.   There is a complete soli-

tude here. I went yesterday to the Imperial Club and found only three persons, who were asleep. I take advantage of my solitude to work at something which I promised my master and which I should like to take to him at Biarritz, but I am progressing very slowly. I have much trouble to do something nowadays. Make me think of showing to you the portrait of a gorilla, which I drew in London. I was on terms of intimacy with him. It is true that he was stuffed. I read only Roman history. The nineteenth volume of M. Thiers's work is more negligently written than the preceding ones, but full of curious things. In spite of his desire to write ill of his hero, he is continually carried away by his involuntary love for him. He says he will finish the twentieth volume in December, and will go then around the world.

CCXLIV.

BIARRITZ, *September* 20, 1861.

DEAR friend, I am here, like a bird on a branch. Usage does not permit one to make projects in advance. Nothing is said

about the time of our departure. Yet the
days are shortening, it is cold after dinner,
and, with the system of doors and windows
invented here, it is impossible to be warm.
All this makes me think that we shall not
stay here long. The sea air does me good.
I breathe easier, but sleep badly. The time
here, as in all imperial residences, is spent
in doing nothing. I work a little, and walk
a great deal. We had a charming promenade, yesterday, along the Pyrenees, near
enough to the mountains in order to see
them in all their beauty, and not near enough
to suffer from their inconveniences. The
Prince Imperial gave a dinner, yesterday, to
a band of children. The Emperor com-
pounded for them, out of seltzer water,
champagne, which had the same effect upon
them as if it were real wine. They were all
drunk in a quarter of an hour, and my ears
are still ill of the noise which they made.
Good-by, dear friend; I have had the temer-
ity to promise to translate for his Majesty
a Spanish memoir, and I have just discovered
that it is terribly difficult to translate.
Good-by.

CCXLV.

PARIS, *November* 2, 1861.

MY eyes are so bad that I did not recognize you at once, the other day. Why do you come into my district without warning me? The man who was with me, asked who the lady was who had such beautiful eyes. I spend all my time working like a nigger for my master, whom I shall see in a week. The perspective of a week of knee breeches frightens me a little. I have a good book for you. My memory is failing, as I sent to the binder a volume whereof I had another copy. You see what you gain by this. When we meet we will talk of metaphysics. I like the subject because it may not be exhausted. Good-by, dear friend.

CCXLVI.

COMPIÈGNE, *November* 17, 1861.

DEAR friend, we are to be here until the 24th. It was his Majesty, the King of Portugal, who prevented us from having the festivals which we were preparing. They

have been postponed and we have been retained here in consequence. We are comfortable here and as independent of one
another as we can be in such a place.

Here are four lions, Highlanders in kilts:
the Duke of Athol, Lord James Murray,
and the Duke's son and nephew. It is
amusing enough to see their eight bare
knees, in a parlor where all the men wear
breeches or tight trousers. Yesterday the
piper of his Grace came, and all four danced
in a way to alarm everybody when they
turned around. But there are ladies whose
crinoline is still more alarming when they
enter a carriage. As the invited women are
permitted not to wear mourning, there are
legs of all colors. I like red stockings.
Despite walks in humid woods and red-hot
drawing-rooms, I have not caught a cold,
but I do not sleep. I was present at the
grand ministerial comedy, wherein one or
two more victims were expected. The faces
were good to observe, the speeches still
more so. What think you of the Emperor's
letter ? I think it is very good. He has his
own way of saying things, and when he talks

as a sovereign he has the art to show that
he is not commonplace, as others are.   I
think that is exactly what this magnanimous
nation wants.   It does not like the commonplace.   Yesterday, Muller's picture, representing Queen Marie Antoinette in prison,
was given to the Empress.   The Prince Imperial asked who this lady was and why she
was not in a palace.   It was explained to
him that she was a Queen of France, and
what a prison was.   Then he ran to the
Emperor and asked him to forgive the Queen
whom he was keeping in prison.   He is an
odd child, sometimes terrible.   He says that
he bows always to the people because they
expelled Louis Philippe, who did not like
them.   He is a charming child.   Good-by,
dear friend.

CCXLVII.

CANNES, *January* 6, 1862.

DEAR friend, I will not tell you of the sun
of Cannes, for fear of grieving you, in the
midst of the snows where you must be now.
What is written to me from Paris makes me

cold.   I have here the society of M. Cousin,
who came here to cure himself of laryngitis,
and who talks like a one-eyed magpie, eats
like an ogre, and is astonished at not being
cured under this beautiful sky, which he
sees for the first time.   He is very amusing,
for he has the good quality of being witty
for everybody.   I suppose that even to his
servant he talks as he would to the most
coquettish duchess.   The natives are spell-
bound, and you may imagine how big their
eyes become when they are told that this
man, who talks well on any subject, has
translated Plato and is the lover of Madame
de Longueville.

I am not doing much here.   I am studying botany in a book and with the grasses
that fall under my hand; but I deplore my
bad sight every instant.   I should have begun this study twenty years ago, when I had
eyes.   It is amusing enough, although su-
premely immoral, since in botany there are
for one lady always six or eight gentlemen
at least, all anxious to offer to her what she
takes from the right and from the left with
much indifference.   I regret very much not

14

to have brought a microscope; yet, with my
spectacles, I have seen stamens court pistils
without being ashamed by my presence.   I
make drawings also, and am reading in a
Russian book the history of a Cossack
named, unfortunately, Bogdan Chmielnick.
With such a name it is not astonishing that
he has remained unknown to us Occidentals,
who remember only names derived from the
Greek or Latin.   How do you govern the
little children who absorb you so much ?   It
seems that it is very amusing to bring up
children.   I have brought up only cats, who
never gave me any satisfaction, excepting
the last one, who had the honor to know
you.   What seems unbearable to me with
children, is the time that one must wait to
know what they have in their brains and
to hear them reason.   It is a pity that the
labor in the intelligence of boys may not be
explained by them and that their ideas come
to them almost unconsciously.   The great
question is to know whether to tell them
silly things, like those which were said to
us, or to talk to them reasonably.   There is
good in both systems.   I have made the ac-

quaintance of a poor cat, who lives in a hut in the woods. I bring meat and bread to him, and as soon as he sees me he comes to me, running with all his might. I regret I cannot take him with me, for he has marvellous instinct. Good-by, dear friend. I hope this letter will find you in good health. I wish you a good and happy new year.

CCXLVIII.

CANNES, *March* 1, 1862.

MY cousin's fête day went out of my head. I remembered it, the other day, when it was too late. We shall talk of it at my return, if you please. It becomes more and more difficult to meet every year, for I have exhausted pins, rings, handkerchiefs, and buttons. It is hard to invent something new. It is not less difficult for novels. I have just read rhapsodies which deserve truly corporal chastisement.

You cannot imagine anything prettier than this country in this weather. All the fields are covered with violets and anemones and a quantity of other flowers, the names

of which I do not know. Good-by, dear
friend. I hope to see you soon. I desire
to find you in the same good condition
which you were in two months ago. Do
not get thin nor fat, do not worry too much,
and think a little of me. Good-by.

CCXLIX.

LONDON, BRITISH MUSEUM,
May 12, 1862.

THE exposition, frankly, resembles a fiasco. It is true that everything is not yet
unpacked, but the building is horrible. Although very large, it does not seem to be
so. One must walk and lose himself in it
to be assured of its extent. Everybody says
that there are beautiful things in it. I find
that the English have made much progress
in taste and art of decoration; we make furniture and wall paper better than they, but
we are in a deplorable way, and if it continues we shall soon be distanced. Our
jury is presided over by a German, who
thinks he is talking English and who is in-
comprehensible to everybody. There is
nothing more absurd than our meetings;

nobody knows what they are about.   Still,
we vote.   The worst is, that there are English manufacturers in our class, and we
shall have to give them medals which they
do not deserve.   I dined, day before yesterday, with Lord Granville.   There were
three small tables in a long gallery.   This
arrangement was to make the conversation
general, but as the people did not know
one another, they hardly talked.   At night
I went to Lord Palmerston's, where was the
Japanese Embassy, which hooked all the women with the big sabres worn at their belts.
I saw many beautiful women and some very
abominable ones; they made a complete
exhibition of their shoulders and breasts,
some admirable, some odious; both with
the same impudence.   I think that the
English have no judgment in these things.
Good-by, dear friend.

CCL.

London, British Museum,
June 6, 1862.
Dear friend, I am beginning to catch a
glimpse of the end of my troubles.   My re-

port to the International Jury, in the purest
Anglo-Saxon, without a single word derived
from the French, was read by me yesterday.
I have to make another report to my government. I think I may leave here about the
20th of this month. You will do well to
write to me before the 15th where you shall
be then and what your intentions are. Decidedly, I think that the exhibition is a
fiasco. The commissioners advertise and
beat the drum, without attracting the crowd.
They need fifty thousand visitors a day and
are far from obtaining them. Fashionable
people do not go, since the price of admis-
sion has been reduced to a shilling. The
restaurant is detestable. Only the American
restaurant is amusing. You are served
there with drinks more or less diabolical,
which are taken with straws: mint julep, for
example, which would raise the dead. All
these drinks are made of gin, more or less
disguised. I am tired of British hospitality
and of its dinners, which seem to have been
made all by the same inexperienced cook.
You cannot imagine how ardent is my desire
to eat soup at home. I do not know if I

told you that my old cook was to quit me
to retire on her lands. She has been with
me for thirty-five years. This annoys me
very much, for nothing is so disagreeable as
new faces. Good-by, dear friend.

CCLI.

PARIS, *July* 17, 1862.

I SHALL not tell you all my regrets. I
wish you had shared them. If you had had
half of them you would have found a way to
make others wait for me. I have had very
annoying days since your departure. My
poor old Caroline died at my house, after
much suffering. After her death, her nieces
came to quarrel about her succession. One
took her cat, which I wanted to keep. She
leaves, it seems, an income of twelve or fifteen hundred francs. It has been demonstrated to me that she could not have amassed
so much money with the wages that I gave
her. But if she robbed me I would sub-
scribe willingly to being robbed in that way
always. I hope to be in Paris when you
arrive there. Madame de Montijo arrived

last week; she is much changed. Nothing
can console her for the death of her daughter, and she is less resigned than on the first
day.   I dined at Saint-Cloud last Thursday
and enjoyed it.   It seemed to me that they
were less devout than people say generally.
They let me gossip about things as I pleased,
without calling me to order.   The little
prince is charming.   He has grown two
inches and is the most charming child I have
ever seen.   It is horribly warm here, but I
do not suffer from it.   Good-by, dear friend.

CCLII.

BAGNÈRES-DE-BIGORRE, HAUTES-PYRÉNÉES,
Saturday, August 16, 1862.

DEAR friend, I have been here for three
days, with M. Panizzi.   The frightful sun
quitted us day before yesterday, and we have
a weather worthy of London—fog and an
imperceptible little rain which drenches you
to the bones.   I met here one of my friends,
who is a physician.   He struck me with his
fist in the back and the chest and discovered
that I had two mortal maladies, of which he

will cure me if I will drink every day two
glasses of warm water, the taste of which is
not bad. Moreover, I bathe in a certain
spring, the water of which is warm, but
agreeable to the skin. It seems to me that
it is doing me a great deal of good. I do
not sleep well, but I have a good appetite.
There is not a crowd here. Englishmen and
prunes failed this year. There are two balls
every week, to which I shall not go, and
concerts, one of which I have heard. The
country is very beautiful. What has become
of you ? Write to me. I would like to
show you the incomparable verdure of this
country and the beauty of the waters, with
which crystal could not compare. It would
be agreeable to talk with you, in the shade
of the big oaks. Good-by, dear friend.

CCLIII.

BAGNÈRES-DE-BIGORRE,
September 1, 1862.

DEAR friend, I thank you for your letter.
The little quarrels and the little affairs of
the province seem so miserable and so pitiful to residents of Paris, that they deplore

the condition of people who have them.   It
is certain, however, that a Parisian, after
a few months in the country, does as the
natives do and becomes completely provincial.   This is sad for human intelligence.
Good-by, dear friend, good-by, and write
me.

CCLIV.

BIARRITZ, VILLA EUGÉNIE,
September 27, 1862.

DEAR friend, if the weather where you are
is similar to ours, you must take advantage
of it and not be in haste to return to the
asphalt of Paris.   I am here, by the seaside,
breathing better than I have breathed for a
long time.   The waters of Bagnères had
begun to hurt me greatly.   I was told then
that it was so much the better.   The fact is,
that as soon as I quitted Bagnères I lived
again ; the sea air, and perhaps also the august food which I eat here, have cured me.
It must be said that there is nothing so abominable as the cooking at Bagnères.   There
are not many persons at the villa and these
only amiable persons, whom I have known

for a long time.   In the city the Americans
predominate.   On reception days, which are
Thursdays, it is necessary to put the Americans of the North on one side and the
Americans of the South on the other side,
otherwise they would devour one another.
We dress on that day.   The rest of the time
the ladies dine in high-necked gowns and
our ugly sex in frock coats.   There is not a
castle in France nor in England where one
feels as free of etiquette.   We have splendid walks in the valleys along the Pyrenees,
and return from them with prodigious appe-
tites.   The sea, which is ordinarily very bad
here, has been surprisingly calm for a week.
The bathers wear strange costumes.   One
woman, who is of the color of a turnip,
dresses in blue and powders her hair.   In
spite of walks and eating, I work a little.   I
have written more than half a volume.   It
is the history of a Cossack hero.   Have you
read Victor Hugo's speech at a dinner of
Belgian book-sellers at Brussels ?   How pitiful it is, that a man having so many beautiful
images at his disposition, will say platitudes
unworthy of an honest man !   There is, in

his comparison of a tunnel with a railway,
more poetry than I have found in any book
that I have read in years; but it lacks common sense.   The twentieth volume of
Thiers's work pleases me.   I like his judgment of Napoleon and other great men.   He
is a little severe on Alexander and on
Cæsar.   Yet there is a good deal of truth
in what he says of the absence of virtue in
Cæsar.   Good-by, dear friend.   Take good
care of yourself and do not sacrifice yourself
too much for others, because they will take
the habit of your doing it, and you may be
obliged to do painfully, some day, what you
do now with pleasure.   Good-by again.

CCLV.

PARIS, *October* 23, 1862.

DEAR friend, I have had a very exciting
time since the beginning of the month.   I
came back from Biarritz with the sovereigns.
We were all ill, having been poisoned, I
think, with verdigris.   The cooks swear that
they mended their pots, but I do not believe
in their protestations.   The fact is, that

fourteen persons at the villa had cramps.   I
was poisoned before with verdigris and know
the symptoms of it.   I remained in Paris a
few days and then went to Marseilles, to in-
stal packet boats for China. You understand
that the ceremony needed my presence.
These packet boats are so beautiful and have
little rooms so well arranged that they give
one the desire to go to China.   I resisted,
however, and was contented with a sun bath
at Marseilles.   You seem to me to be too
much moved by Victor Hugo's speech.
They are words without ideas.   Read a letter of Madame de Sévigné, to return to good
prose.   I would like to know your projects.
I will tell you mine.   I shall go to Compiègne about the 8th of next month and remain there until after the Empress's fête;
that it, until the 18th or 20th.   Before or
after that time, may I not see you ?   It
seems to me that the country must be very
cold and very damp at present, and that you
should think of returning.   Good-by, dear
friend; I hope you are in good appetite and
health.

CCLVI.

PARIS, *November* 5, 1862.

DEAR friend, I am invited to Compiègne until the 18th. I shall be in Paris on the 10th until three o'clock and hope to see you. I disapprove of your new literary taste. I am reading a book which may amuse you; it is the history of the revolt of the Netherlands, by Motley. There are no less than five thick volumes. Although not too well written, they are interesting. He has a great deal of anti-Catholic and anti-monarchical partiality, but he has made extensive researches and is a man of talent, although an American. I have a cold and a pain in my lungs. You will learn some day that I have ceased to breathe for the lack of viscera. This ought to make you very amiable toward me. Good-by, dear friend.

CCLVII.

CANNES, *December* 5, 1862.

DEAR friend, I have arrived here between two overflows, and for four days I have thought that there was no more sun, even at Cannes. When it begins to rain here, it is not a joke. The plain between Cannes and the Esterel was changed into a lake. Still, in this deluge, the air was soft and agreeable. Happily, this condition did not last long. The sun reappeared, radiant, three days ago, and since then I live with my windows open and am almost too warm. Before leaving Paris I consulted a great physician, for I imagined I was in a very bad state, since my return from Compiègne, and I wanted to know when I should prepare for my funeral. I am well pleased with having consulted him; first, because he said this ceremony would not take place as soon as I apprehended; second, because he explained to me, anatomically and very clearly, the cause of my ills. I thought my heart was ill; not at all. It is my lung. It is true that I will never be cured; but there is a way of not suffering from it, and that is a great deal, if not the principal thing.

You cannot form an idea of the beauty of the country, after all these rains. There are May roses everywhere. The jessamines are beginning to bloom, as also a quantity of wild flowers, all very pretty. I would like to take a course of botany with you in the woods. I have received here the last book of M. Gustave Flaubert, who wrote " Madame Bouverie," which you have read, I think, although you would not confess that you have. I thought he had a great deal of talent which he was wasting under the pretext of realism. He has just written a new novel, which he calls " Salammbo." In any other place than Cannes I would not have opened this volume. It is a history of Carthage, several years before the second Punic war. The author has acquired a sort of false erudition by reading Bouillet, and he accompanies it with a lyrism copied from the worst phrases of Victor Hugo. There are pages in it which will please you, doubtless, since, like all persons of your sex, you like emphasis. For me it is hateful, and the book has made me furious. Good-by, dear friend. I hope winter will not treat you badly and that you will take care to escape colds. Is your little niece still amiable ? Do not spoil her, so that she shall not be miserable later.

CCLVIII.

CANNES, *January* 3, 1863.

DEAR friend, I began the year badly in my bed with painful lumbago.   This is what one earns in these beautiful climates where, as long as the sun is on the horizon, one may imagine one's self in summer, but immediately after sunset comes a quarter of an hour of humid cold which penetrates the marrow of one's bones.   It is as in Rome, with the exception that here one gets rheumatism and there fever.   My back regained some of its elasticity to-day.

You are wrong not to read " Salammbo." It is true that it is perfectly crazy, but after all there is a great deal of talent in it. Good-by; do not forget me.

CCLIX.

CANNES, *January* 28, 1863.

DEAR friend, I was preparing to go to Paris, when I had a new attack of spasms in the stomach.   The physician tells me that if I return to Paris before being entirely cured,

15

I shall surely fall lower than I was, and so
I shall remain here for a fortnight.   The
weather is admirable; still, this climate is a
little treacherous.   I should not be deceived
by it.   As long as the sun is on the horizon
one imagines it is June; five minutes later
comes a penetrating dampness.   It is because I have admired too long the beautiful
sunsets that I have fallen ill.   Around us,
a quantity of snow has fallen, and nothing
can be more beautiful than the view of our
mountains, all white, surrounding our little
green oasis.

There has been a tragedy in our neighbor-
hood.   A pretty English miss was burned
at a ball.   Her mother, in trying to save
her, was burned also.   Both died in three or
four days.   The husband, who was burned
also, is still ill.   This is the eighteenth
woman of my acquaintance to whom this
has happened.   Why do you wear a crinoline ?   You ought to set a good example.
One has only to turn before the chimney,
or look at one's self in the glass—there is
always a glass above the chimney—to be
roasted alive.   It is true that one dies but

once and that it is a great pleasure to show
a monstrous back.   But who is deceived by
a balloon full of air ?   Why do you not put
a metallic curtain before your chimney ?
Good-by, dear friend.

CCLX.

PARIS, *April* 26, 1863.

DEAR friend, as I was not counting on
your manner of travelling like a turtle, I did
not write to you at Genoa.   I am addressing
my letter to Florence, where I hope you will
stay for a time.   It is the city of Italy which
has best preserved its characteristics of the
Middle Age.   Be careful not to catch cold.
As for Rome, it is so long since I have
been there that I am unable to give you advice about it.   Only, I would recommend
that you should not be out in the air at sunset, because you might catch the fever.
You should go to the Saint Peter cathedral
a quarter of an hour before the angelus and
wait there until the strange humidity of the
atmosphere, which happens then, shall have

passed. There is nothing more beautiful than this great church at the close of day. It is sublime, truly. Think of me there. Some rainy day, go to the Catacombs. Go to one of the small corridors leading into the subterranean streets; put out your candle and remain alone for three or four minutes. You will tell me the sensations which came to you. I should be pleased to make the experiment with you; but then you would not feel, perhaps, the same thing. It never happened to me to see at Rome what I had intended to see, because I was attracted at every street corner by something unexpected, and it is a great pleasure to yield to that sensation. I recommend also that you should not visit too many palaces. Most of them are over-praised. Be preoccupied especially by frescoes and by views of nature. I recommend to you the view of Rome and of its surroundings from Saint Peter in Montorio. There is a very beautiful fresco of the Vatican. See, at the Capitol, the Wolf of the Republic, which bears the trace of the lightning that struck it in the time of Cicero. I believe that you shall

not be able to see a hundredth part of what
you should see, in the little time that you
will have to give to your voyage.   I regret
your departure.   I will say that you have
done well to take advantage of the oppor-
tunity to see Rome.   There remains only
the question of damages due me, which I
pray you to keep in mind.   I hope that you
think of it sometimes.   There is not a beautiful place which I have seen, without regret-
ting my inability to associate you with it in
my memory.   Good-by, dear friend; write
to me often, a few lines only; enjoy yourself well and come back in good condition.
Good-by.

CCLXI.

PARIS, *May* 20, 1863.

DEAR friend, I write to you with an
abominable grippe.   For a fortnight I have
been coughing instead of sleeping.   The
only remedy is to take laudanum, and this
gives me headache.   In brief, I feel weak and
like going to the devil.   I hope it is not the
same with you.   I think I have told you to

take good care against the humidity, which, in the country where you are, goes with sunset. Take care to be never cold, even if you should be too warm. I envy you for being in that beautiful land, where melancholy is sweet and agreeable, but I wish that, to make the comparison better, you went for a week to Naples. Of all transitions, it is the harshest and the most amusing I know. Moreover, it has the advantage of comedy after tragedy. I do not know if the art of cooking has progressed in the states of the Holy Father. In my time it was the abomination of desolation. It may be that political revolutions have levelled the kitchens of Rome and Naples, and that, gourmet as you are, you will find them both bad.

I hoped that you would tell me some stories, or at least your impressions. It always pleases me to know how things appear to you. Do not forget to see the statue of Pompey, which is probably the one at the foot of which Cæsar was murdered; and if you discover the shop of a man named Cades, who sells false antiques and pottery, buy me an intaglio of some old stone.

CCLXII.

PARIS, *Friday, June* 12, 1863.

DEAR friend, I learn with great pleasure your return to France. I hope that you will be here next week and that I shall see you before my departure, on the 21st, for Fontainebleau. You do not write of your health. I suppose that, despite the bad Papal cooking, you are in good condition.

CCLXIII.

PALACE OF FONTAINEBLEAU,
Thursday, July 2, 1863.

DEAR friend, I would have liked to reply sooner to your letter, which gave me great pleasure, but one here has the time to do nothing, and the days elapse with a prodigious rapidity. The grand and principal occupation is to sleep, eat and drink. I succeed in eating and drinking, but not in sleeping. There are a number of people here, less official than usual. We walk at times in the woods, after dining on the grass like the milliners of the Rue Saint Denis.

Several large cases were brought here, day before yesterday, from his Majesty, the Emperor of Cochin-China. They were opened in one of the yards. In the big cases were smaller ones, painted red and gold and covered with cockroaches. The first contained two very yellow elephant's tusks and two rhinoceros horns, plus a package of mildewed cinnamon. There came from all this, inconceivable odors, half rancid butter and half spoiled fish. In the other case were narrow stuffs, resembling gauze, in ugly colors, all more or less dirty and, moreover, mildewed. Gold medals had been promised, but they were not there, and they remain, probably, in Cochin-China. The inference is that the grand Emperor of Cochin-China is a swindler. All the ladies are sunburnt. We are going to a Spanish dinner in the forest to-day and I am charged with the duty of making the ladies eat raw onions. They would faint at the mere name of that vegetable. I have given strict orders that they shall not be warned, and, when they shall have eaten the raw onions, I will make my confession myself.

CCLXIV.

LONDON, *August* 12, 1863.

DEAR friend, I thank you for your letter, which I was expecting impatiently. I thought London would be empty, and that was the first impression which I felt, in fact. But I perceived, after two days, that the great ant-hill was still inhabited, and especially, alas! that people ate there as much as last year. Is not the slowness of dinners in this country inhuman? It takes even appetite from you. One has to remain two hours and a half at table, and if one adds the half hour which the men leave to women to talk ill of them, it is always eleven o'clock before the men return to the drawing-room.

The great men seem to me to have grown old since my last visit. Lord Palmerston has abandoned his false set of teeth, and is much changed thereby. He has retained his mutton chops and looks like a gorilla who is gay. Lord Russell is not in such good humor. The great beauties of the season have gone, but they were not highly praised. The gowns seemed to me, as always, very mediocre and mussy; but nothing resists the air of this country. My throat is an evidence of it.

CCLXV.

PARIS, *August* 30, 1863.

I AM going, to-morrow, to Biarritz with Panizzi. We are invited by our gracious sovereign, who shall be our host for I do not know how long. I shall go to Cannes in October. I have an extremely curious book, which I will lend to you if you be good to me. It is the relation, made by a fool, of a suit in the seventeenth century. A nun of his Majesty's family "*faceval*' *amore*" with a Milanese gentleman, and, as there were other nuns whom it displeased, she killed them with the aid of her lover. It is very edifying. Read " Une Saison à Paris," by Madame de ———. She is a person full of candor, who felt a very great necessity to please his Majesty, and said it to him at a ball, in tones so categoric and so clear that nobody in the world, except you, would have misunderstood her. He was so stupe-

fied that he did not know what to reply, and
it was only three days afterward that he
comprehended.   I imagine you making the
sign of the cross and a horrified grimace.
Have you read Renan's " Life of Jesus " ?
Probably not.   It is a blow with an axe on
the edifice of Catholicism.   The author is
so frightened by his own audacity in denying the divinity, that he loses himself in
hymns of admiration and of adoration.   It
is interesting.

CCLXVI.

CANNES, *October* 19, 1863.

HAVE you read the command of the
Bishop of Tulle, to all the religious of his
diocese, to recite Aves in honor of M.
Renan, or, rather, to prevent the devil from
taking away everything because of M.
Renan's book ?   Since you are reading the
letters of Cicero, you must find that the
people of his time were wittier than ours.
I am ashamed whenever I think of our nineteenth century, so inferior to its predeces-
sors.   I leave you, to go fishing with a line,

or rather to see others fish, for I never could catch a fish. The best of it is, that they make by the seaside an excellent soup for those who like oil and garlic. I suppose you count yourself among them.

CCLXVII.

PALACE OF COMPIÈGNE,
November 16, 1863, *at night.*

DEAR friend, since my arrival here, I have led the agitated life of an impressario. I have been an author, an actor, and a theatrical manager. We played with success a play, somewhat immoral, the subject of which I shall relate to you at my return. We have had magnificent sky-rockets, and a woman who wanted to see them too closely was killed. We have had long walks. I shall remain in Paris until the first days of December and then return to Cannes, which I left in bloom. It is impossible to imagine anything more beautiful than its fields of jessamine and of tuberoses. You write to me so laconically that you never reply to my questions. You have a way of doing only what

you want, which confounds me always; you
jest, you promise. When I read your letters
I seem to hear you; I am disarmed, but furious in fact. You do not even tell me what
is becoming of the charming child who in-
terests you so much. I pray you not to
make her as silly as most women of our
time. There is here Miss ——, who is a
beautiful girl, five feet four inches high, with
all the gentleness of a grisette and an amusing mingling of easy manners and honest
timidity. We were fearing that the second
part of a comedy would not be equivalent
to the first part. She said: " It will be all
right. We will show our legs in the ballet."
Note that her legs are like pipe-stems and
her feet not aristocratic. Good-by, dear
friend.

CCLXVIII.

PARIS, *Friday, December* 12, 1863.

DEAR friend, you complain of having a
cold, and you do not know what that is.
Only one person in Paris has a cold, and that
is I. I spend my life coughing and stifling,
and if it continues you shall have to give

my funeral oration.   Do you know Aristophanes ?   I have translated for you one of
his works.   There are things in it which will
grieve your prudery, but they will interest
you.

CCLXIX.

CANNES, *January* 12, 1864.

DEAR friend, I was ill as soon as I arrived.
I brought from Paris an abominable cold.
I do not know what would have become of
me if I had remained there.   At times, the
east wind brings a bit of snow taken from
the Alps, but we are in a privileged oasis.
I represent to myself a man of Marseilles in
the snow, as a cat on the ice with nutshells
on its paws.   I am charmed that Aristophanes had the honor of pleasing you.   You
ask if the Athenian women were present at
theatrical performances.   There are men of
learning who say yes; there are others who
say no.   If you had seen Karagueuz when
you were in the Orient you would have
found, doubtless, many women there.   In
the Orient to-day, and formerly, in anti-
quity, there was none of the prudery which

prevails at present. What is the name of
the comedy wherein Euripides is dressed
as a woman ? Do you understand the part
of the Scythe policeman ? The lack of
reserve with which Aristophanes talks of
the gods on the day of their festival is
more extraordinary than all the rest. The
same thing happened in the first days of
Christianity. Comedy was played in the
churches. There was the mass of the fools
and the mass of the ass, the text of which is
extant in a very curious manuscript. The
wicked have spoiled everything by doubting.
When everybody had faith all was permissible. Besides the silly things which Aristophanes throws into his plays, like salt,
there are choruses of most beautiful poetry.
I recommend "The Clouds" to you, if you
have not read it. It is, in my opinion, the
best play which has been retained of his.
There is in it a dialogue of the just and the
unjust, which is in the most elevated style.
I think that there is some truth in his reproaches to Socrates. The man who proves
to everybody, as Socrates did, that he is an
ass, is a plague. Good-by, dear friend.

CCLXX.

CANNES, *February* 17, 1864.

DEAR friend, since you have taken the trouble to read Aristophanes, I forgive you your ways and your prudery in reading him. Admit only that he is very witty, and it would be a great pleasure to see one of his comedies. I do not know what the opinion of the men of learning at present is on the presence of women at the theatre. It is probable that there were periods of tolerance and of intolerance in the same country, but the women never went on the stage. Their parts were played by men, which was easy because all the actors wore masks.

I am very ill, dear friend, and feel that I am going to a better world, through a path which is not very agreeable. I have very painful spasms. I cannot sleep. I have no appetite and feel very feeble. What will become of me when, instead of a magnificent sky, I shall have the leaden sky of Paris and rain and fog in permanence! I am thinking of returning there at the end of this month,

if I have the strength, for I am somewhat
ashamed not to be doing any of my official
trades.

CCLXXI.

Friday, March 18, 1864.

I AM writing to you in the Luxembourg,
while the Bishop of Rouen is damning im-
piety.   If you have not seen the new halls
in the Louvre, where vases and terra-cottas
are classified, you would do well to go there.
I offer to you the accompaniment of my
lights.   You shall see there very beautiful
things, and others to interest you, though
they might shock your prudery.   Appoint
your day and hour.

CCLXXII.

Wednesday, April 13, 1864.

DEAR friend, I have regretted much your
departure.   You should have bade me farewell once more.   You would have found me
ill.   I suffer, in spite of arsenic and the rest.

16

I hardly go out; yet desired to see my masters, who are in good health. This visit gave me the advantage of seeing at their best the new fashions, which I do not admire. This is a sign of old age. I cannot bear the new styles of hair-dress. There is not one woman who dresses her hair for her face; all take the style of wigged heads. One of my friends introduced me to his wife, who is young and pretty. She had a foot of rouge, painted eyelashes, and was powdered. This horrified me. Have you read About's book? It is at your service. I do not know if it is successful. Perhaps the clericals were sensible enough not to excommunicate it, which is the surest means of selling a book. I promise myself never to go to the academy again, except to collect my wages, eighty-three francs, thirty-three centimes every month. I am absorbed by a history of Peter the Great. He was an abominable man, surrounded by abominable scoundrels. That amuses me.

CCLXXIII.

London, British Museum,
July 21, 1864.

DEAR friend, you have guessed where I was. I have been here since the last time that we met. I spend my time, from eight o'clock in the evening to midnight, in dining out, and the morning in seeing books and statues, or in writing my great article on the son of Peter the Great, which I have a great wish to entitle, " The Danger of Being Stupid." For the moral of my work is, that one must be witty. I think that you will find here and there, in a score of pages, some interesting things, notably how Peter the Great was deceived by his wife. I have translated with a great deal of trouble and care the love-letters of his wife to her lover, who was impaled in the bargain. They are really better than one could expect of the time and country where she wrote. But love achieves marvels. The misfortune is that she did not know orthography, which makes it difficult for grammarians like me to guess what she means.

They are talking of nothing here but the marriage of Lady Florence Paget.   It is impossible to see a prettier figure or a more delicate body, too small and too delicate for my particular taste.   She was celebrated for her flirtations.   Ellice's nephew, Chaplin, of whom I have spoken to you often, a tall fellow twenty-five years old, with an income of twenty-five thousand pounds sterling, fell in love with her.   She hesitated for a long time, then engaged herself, and received jewels and six thousand pounds sterling to pay her dressmaker's bills.   Last Friday, they went together to the park and to the opera.   Saturday morning she went out alone to the church of St. George, and there married Lord Hastings, a young man of her age, very homely, having two little defects; to wit, gambling and drink.   After the religious ceremony they went to the country.   At the first station she wrote to the marquis, her father: "Dear Pa, as I knew you would never consent to my marriage with Lord Hastings, I was wedded to him to-day.   I remain, yours, etc."   She wrote to Chaplin: "Dear Harry, when you receive this I shall

be the wife of Lord Hastings.   Forget
yours very truly, Florence.'' Poor Chaplin,
six feet tall, yellow haired, and in despair!
Good-by, dear friend.

CCLXXIV.

PARIS, *October* 1, 1864.

DEAR friend, I am here, belated by my
proofs, and you see that they need careful
correction.   I shall start irrevocably on the
8th.   I shall sleep at Bayonne, and be at
Madrid on the 11th.   I do not know how
long I shall stay there.   The Pope has prohibited in Rome the painting of French
signs.   They must be all Italian.   There is,
on the Corso, a Madame Bernard, who sells
gloves and garters.   They have forced her
to call herself Signora Bernardi.   If I were
the government I would not permit this.
There is a great scandal here, which amuses
perverse people, but I shall not relate it to
you for fear of making you angry.   Good-
by, dear friend.

CCLXXV.

MADRID, *October* 24, 1864.

CAN you imagine the misery of people living on an elevated plateau, exposed to all the winds, having nothing with which to warm themselves except *braseros,* very primitive pieces of furniture that give one the choice of freezing or suffocating ? I find that civilization here has made much progress; this does not embellish Madrid. The women have adopted your absurd hats and wear them in absurd fashion. The bulls have lost much of their merit, and the men who kill them are ignorant and cowardly. Where are you, what are you doing ? Write to me quickly.

CCLXXVI.

CANNES, *December* 4, 1864.

DEAR friend, I find not a word from you, which grieves me a great deal. I have another grievance against you. You have given me all sorts of trouble with your handkerchiefs. I discovered, at last, half a dozen Nipi handkerchiefs, very ugly. I took them, although everybody said they were out of fashion; but I was obeying orders. I hope you have received them. You wanted them embroidered. There was not one more in Madrid than the six I sent you. Good-by, dear friend. Write to me and tell me what your projects are for this winter.

CCLXXVII.

CANNES, *December* 30, 1864.

WHAT do you think of the Pope's encyclical letter ? There is here a bishop, a man of wit and of common sense, who veils his face. It is truly pitiful to be in an army whose general exposes it to defeat. I am without news from my publisher. Are there new novels for Christmas ? I mean English novels, for this is the time when they come into bloom. Good-by, dear friend. I have to write thirty-five letters; I began with you; I wish you all the prosperities.

CCLXXVIII.

CANNES, *January* 20, 1865.

DEAR friend, have you received your execrable Nipi handkerchiefs ? I learned that the person who was to take them to Paris, having been elected a member of the Cortes, had remained in Madrid and had given the handkerchiefs to Madame de Montijo, who did not know what they were. Spaniards are not brilliant in making clear explanations. I have written to the Countess Montijo to give the package to our ambassador, who will send it to you by the French mail. I hope you will receive it before my letter, but I do not wish to take again the responsibility of your commissions, which force me to make more prose than they are worth. The best thing that you can do is to throw the handkerchiefs in the fire.

We have here a detestable winter, not cold, but rainy. I take great pleasure in reading the letters of the bishops. There are few lawyers as subtle as these gentlemen. The most subtle among them is one who makes the Pope say precisely the re-

verse of his encyclical. I know nothing of my works, and if you have learned something about them I should be obliged if you would let me know. The number of Englishmen becomes day by day more and more frightful. They have built on the seashore a hotel almost as large as the Louvre, and it is always full. One cannot go out without meeting young misses in Garibaldi jackets, with impossible feather-decked hats, pretending to make sketches. There are croquet and archery parties, where come a hundred and twenty persons. I regret the good old times when nobody came. I have made the acquaintance of a tame sea-gull, which I feed with fish. It catches the fish in the air, always head first, and swallows some bigger than my neck. Do you remember an ostrich of the Jardin des Plantes whom you strangled, almost, with lozenges, in the time when you embellished the place with your presence ? Good-by, dear friend. I expect to return to Paris soon and find you there.

CCLXXIX.

CANNES, *April* 14, 1865.

DEAR friend, I was waiting to be cured before writing to you; but in spite of the beautiful weather, in spite of all possible care, I am always the same; that is, very ill.   I cannot accustom myself to this life of suffering and I have neither courage nor resignation.   The sky here is magnificent.   What are you doing this spring ?   Shall I find you in Paris ?   So your friend, Paradol, becomes an academician.   Ampère has written a very bad history of Cæsar in verse; you can comprehend all the allusions which Paradol will make to this work, forgotten now by everybody.   You know, perhaps, that William Brougham, brother of Lord Brougham and his successor to the peerage, has just been caught in a very ugly swindle.   This creates a great scandal here among the English colony.   The old Lord Brougham retains his equanimity.   He is, of course, entirely innocent of any wrong.   I am reading, against sleeplessness, a book by Charles Lambert, who demolishes the holy King

David and the Bible. It seems to me to be very ingenious and amusing enough. The clericals have succeeded in making popular serious and pedantic works which, fifteen years ago, would not have attracted anybody's attention. Renan has gone to Palestine to make new studies of landscapes. Peyrat and Charles Lambert are writing books more serious and more learned, which sell like hot cakes, according to my bookseller. Good-by, dear friend.

CCLXXX.

PARIS, *July* 5, 1865.

DEAR friend, I was beginning to fear that you had been devoured by some bear. I thought you were in the Tyrol, when your letter came. It is better to travel, I think, in the long days than in the fall, but nothing prevents you from going to Munich in September. Only you should take care to take warm clothing with you, for the weather changes very suddenly in that big, ugly, and very high plain of Munich. You should go to the Hotel Bavaria and not to Maullich's, where I was robbed of my boots. A guide will show you everything worthy of attention. The paintings in the palace are interesting enough, but you need special permission to see them. You should see, in the Museum of Antiques, the front of the temple of Egina and the marble group of which I spoke to you. The Greek vases are very curious. The frescoes of Cornelius will make you shrug your shoulders. There is nothing at Innsbruck except the landscape and the bronze statues of the cathedral. In all these places you may be sure to find a bed and a tolerable dinner. Buy green stockings at Salzburg or at Innsbruck, if you find any that fit you. The Bavarian legs are as big as my body. Good-by, dear friend; take good care of yourself and enjoy yourself.

CCLXXXI.

LONDON, BRITISH MUSEUM,
August 23, 1865.

DEAR friend, I have been here for about six weeks. I have had some terrible dinners. It seems to me that Lord Palmerston

is aging remarkably, in spite of his success
at the elections. I have spent three days
with his probable successor, Gladstone. I
find pleasure, always, in observing the varieties of human nature. Here they are so
different from ours that one cannot understand how it happens. Gladstone has seemed
to me to be, under certain aspects, a man
of genius, under others, a child. There are
elements in him of the child, the statesman,
and the madman. There were five or six
deans at his house, and every morning the
guests regaled themselves with a short prayer
in common. What seemed preferable to
everything was a sort of badly cooked bread,
which is drawn from the oven at breakfast
time and which is not digested in a day.
Add to this the ale of Wales, which is celebrated. I suppose you have noticed that
the hair now should be red. Nothing is
easier in this country. There has been nobody here for a month. There is not a single
horse in Rotten Row. I like well enough a
large city in this lethargic state. I take advantage of it to see lions. I went yesterday
to the Crystal Palace and spent an hour look-

ing at a chimpanzee, almost as tall as a child ten years old, and so similar to a child in his actions that I felt humiliated by his incontestable relationship. I have written an article on the " History of Cæsar." I shall return to Paris next week. I hope to find you there. I have enough of London. I have had for an instant the thought of going to Scotland, but I should have fallen among hunters, a race which I hold in abhorrence. Good-by, dear friend; keep me posted about your movements; return from the Tyrol with green stockings, I pray you; but I dare you to return with Tyrolean legs.

CCLXXXII.

PARIS, *September* 12, 1865.

DEAR friend, I have been here for several days. I came through Boulogne, and while they were fastening our boat to the quay there was such a crowd that I asked myself what could be so interesting in our arrival. You should warn the English ladies that they make a great exhibition of legs, and more, in walking on the quay's edge when

the tide is low.   My modesty has suffered
from this exhibition.

Paris is emptier than ever, this year.   It
pleases me in that state.   I rise and go to
bed late; I read a great deal and hardly get
out of my dressing-gown.   It is a Japanese
gown with embroideries on a jonquil-yellow
background, more brilliant than the electric
light.   I was not bored very much in England.   I wrote for the " Journal des Savants "
an article on the "Cæsar " about which I have
spoken to you already.   You know all the
good that I think of the author and of his
book; but you understand the difficulties of
my work, not wishing to pass for a courtier,
nor to say disagreeable things.   I think I
got out of the dilemma well enough.   I took
for a text the idea that the Republic had
come to its end and that the Roman people
was going to the devil, from which Cæsar
rescued it.   As the thesis is true and easily
supported, I wrote variations on that air.
Manners are still progressing.   The son of a
prince has just died in Rome.   He had a
brother and sisters who were not rich.   He
was an ecclesiastic, a monsignor, and had an

income of two hundred thousand pounds.
He bequeathed everything to his secretary.
It is as if Nicomede had bequeathed his
kingdom to Cæsar.   I would bet that you
do not understand.   It seems to me that
Boulogne is becoming more beautiful.   I
saw fishwomen there coquettishly dressed ;
but what English women there are, and what
hats they wear ! Good-by, dear friend.   I
am going for two days to Trouville.

CCLXXXIII.

PARIS, *October* 13, 1865.

DEAR friend, I found your letter yesterday at my return from Biarritz.   The first
welcome of my native city was not amiable.
I had, last night, one of my longest attacks
of spasms.   It comes, I suppose, from the
change of air, or it may be the result of a
journey of fourteen hours in a railway train.
This morning I feel better.   I have lamen-
table letters from people about nothing but
cholera.   Nobody thinks of it here, and I
think that, except drunkards, none suffered
seriously.   If the cholera had begun in Paris

no one would have paid any attention to it.
The cowardice of the people of Marseilles
was necessary to warn us of it.   I think I
have told you my theory on cholera.   One
dies of it only when one wishes to die, and
it is so well bred that it never calls on you
without sending its visiting card in advance,
as the Chinese do.

At Biarritz, we had a visit from the King
and Queen of Portugal.   The King is a very
timid German student.   The Queen is charming.   She resembles the Princess Clotilde,
but is more beautiful.   She is a revised
edition.   Her complexion is of a white and
of a rose, rare, even in England.   It is true
that her hair is red, but it is a very dark red.
She is amiable and polite.   There were, in
their train, a certain number of male and
female caricatures, apparently picked up in
a second-hand shop.   The Minister of Portugal recited a tirade about me to her Majesty, which she heard with much grace-
fulness.   The Emperor introduced me to
the King, who extended his hand and looked
at me with two large, round, surprised eyes.
Another personage, M. de Bismarck, pleased

17

me more.   He is a big German, very polite,
who is not naïve.   He seems to be absolutely
destitute of " *gemuth*," but he is full of wit.
He conquered my heart.   He brought with
him a wife, who has the largest feet on the
Rhine, and a daughter who walks in her
mother's footsteps.   Please tell me what I
may read, among the beautiful things that
have been written since I have ceased to live
among the most witty people in the universe.
I would like to see you.

CCLXXXIV.

Paris, *November* 8, 1865.

I would have liked to go to Cannes; but
I was asked to remain for the first festivals
at Compiègne, and the request was made
with such good grace that I could not refuse.

I returned from Biarritz in very good
health, but after three days I felt all the
rigor of a change of climate.   I have been
better for a few days.   I think that Compiègne will hurt me a great deal, but I shall
go to the south of France as soon as I can.

You cannot imagine the scandal of Prin-

cess Anna's marriage, nor the comic rage of
the Faubourg Saint-Germain.   There is not
a family having a daughter, who did not
count on the Duc de Mouchy.   The great
question is, " If they make calls, shall we
send cards to them ?"   There is, at this
moment, a marriageable girl with several
millions in her pocket and some fifty others
to come.   She is a very pretty girl, somewhat mysterious, a daughter of M. Heine,
who died this year; an adopted daughter,
be it understood, whose origin no one
knows.   But for millions the finest names
of France, Germany and Italy are prepared
to ally themselves with all sorts of platitudes.
Adopted children are agreeable to the god-
dess Fortune.   The Greeks of to-day call
them children of the mind.

There is only one man of genius at present: Ponson du Terrail.   Have you read one
of his feuilletons ?   No one handles as he
does, crime and assassination.   It is delightful.   If you were here I would like to shake
your orthodoxy by making you read a curious book on Moses, David, and Saint Paul.
It is not an idyll, like Renan's, but a dis-

sertation, too much larded with Greek and Hebrew. It is worth reading. But you do not like conversations like this, and you are right. There are other things to say to you. Good-by, dear friend; I have a great desire to see you.

CCLXXXV.

CANNES, *January* 2, 1866.

DEAR friend, I did not know where to write to you. That is why I did not write. You lead such an errant life that one does not know where to catch you. You have taken the habit of subalternizing yourself. You are at times the victim of the sea lions, and oftener the victim of that child whom you love, so that there is no way of seeing you, as in the good old times when we were so glad to be together. Do you remember?

I came here in a pretty bad state of health, after a week at Compiègne. They tried to keep me, but I resisted heroically, and fled here. The sun has produced its ordinary effect. How is it that, liking to travel as

you do, you do not spend your winters at
Pisa, or in some place where the great arbiter
of human healths, my lord of the sun, is?
I think that if it were not for him I would
be under the earth.   All my contemporaries
hasten to precede me there.   Last year was
rough for a little circle of my friends.   We
dined together once a month: I am the sole
survivor.   This is my grave reproach against
the Great Mechanic.   Why do not men fall,
like leaves, in one season?   Your Father
Hyacinth will not fail to say silly things.
He will say, " O, man, what are ten years,
a century!"   What is eternity to me?
What is important for me is a small number
of days.   Why are they so bitter?

Only a quarter of the ordinary visitors at
Cannes are here this year.   Reason: a Parisian ate three lobsters and died of cholera.
The land was at once placed under suspicion,
and the mayors of Nice and of Cannes conceived the bad idea of denying, in the newspapers, that the cholera had come.   So
everybody believed that it had.   Several of
my friends have been as heroic as I, and we
form a small colony which dispenses with

the crowd.   Good-by, dear friend.   I send
you my best and most tender wishes.

CCLXXXVI.

CANNES, *February* 20, 1866.

DEAR friend, you charge me with laziness
and you are the very model of it !   You live
in Paris and talk of things with honest folk,
and might keep me informed of what happens in the great city; and you never relate
anything.   Is it true that the crinoline is
proscribed and that between the gown and
the skin nothing but the shirt is worn ?   If
that is so, shall I recognize you when I arrive
in Paris ?   I remember an old man who said
to me, when I was young, that when he went
into a drawing-room where were women
without panniers and without powder, he
imagined seeing chambermaids assembled
in the absence of their mistresses.   I am not
sure that one can be a woman without a
crinoline.

You say nothing to me of Ponsard's play.
He has preserved the tradition of the Cor-
nelian verse, somewhat emphatic, but large,

sonorous, and good.   I imagine that the
fashionable people admire this, as they admire the sermons of the Abbé Lacordaire,
buying a cat in a bag because it is said to
be as it should be.

I have just read a little book on the religions of Asia, which is very interesting.   It
seems that in Persia one is hardly a Mussul-
man.   New religions are making there, and
renewals of antique superstitions.   If I am
in Paris when the question in which you are
interested comes to the Senate, I will vote
as you advise me.   I expect to be in Paris
at the beginning of next month.   What is
said and done at present seems to be more
and more silly.   We are much more absurd
than they were in the middle ages.   Good-
by, dear friend.

CCLXXXVII.

PARIS, *April* 9, 1866.

DEAR friend, is it not a fatality that you
should depart when I arrive ?   Fortunately,
you will return soon.   I have been here
since Saturday night.   I left, hardly breath-

ing, and the travel made me worse. We
had a terrible storm last night, which I hope
will do me good. Try to cover yourself
with all your furs and to leave the chimney
corner as seldom as possible and only when
the days are sunny. I have become so sensitive to the cold, or, rather, the cold hurts
me so much, that I imagine hell is the com-
partment of the " bolge " in Dante. Happily, I am told, the crinoline is out of fashion, which puts your legs and the rest under
shelter. I went out yesterday for an hour
and saw a woman without a crinoline, but
with skirts so extraordinary that I was stup-
efied. They seemed to me to be made of
pasteboard with furbelows. They made a
good deal of noise on the asphalt.

It is your habit to do the very reverse of
common mortals, and, as the country will
soon be agreeable, I presume that you are
to return to Paris. Have the kindness to
advise me of your intentions.

I am asking myself if I shall go, Thursday, to the Academy to aid in the making
of an Immortal. Between Henri Martin
and Cuvillier-Fleury or M. de Champagny,

one does not know what to do. However, the latter is a little too clerical for me, and I am angry with him for writing on Roman history in newspaper style. Have you read anything by Cuvillier-Fleury ? If you have, tell me what you think of him. If you give me a reward I shall vote for whomever you designate.

The modern English novels bore me mortally. They were our great resource at Cannes. Do you know anything which may keep company with a poor devil unable to go out after dark ? Good-by, dear friend; think a little of me.

CCLXXXVIII.

PARIS, *June* 24, 1866.

WHAT becomes of you ? It seems that the cholera prevails at Amiens. I do not know what is reserved for us at Luxembourg, and perhaps the senatus-consult, with which we are threatened, will force me to remain here till the end of the month. I have bought, to console myself, the twenty-seven volumes of the " Mémoires du

XVIIIème Siècle,'' which I shall have bound.
Is there anything in them that you would
like to have ? I received, with astonishment, the book which you sent back to me.
I was afraid that you had added it to those
which you have already taken from me.
When will you come and take another ? In
spite of the heat, I am quite ill.

You asked me, the other day, where I got
acquainted with the dialect of the Bohe-
mians. I had so many things to say to you
that I forgot to reply. I learned it from M.
Borrow; his book is one of the most curious
that I have read. What he tells of the Bo-
hemians is perfectly true, and his personal
observations are entirely in accord with
mine, except upon one point. In his quality
as a clergyman, he may have been mistaken
where, in my quality as a Frenchman and a
layman, I could make conclusive experi-
ments. It is strange that this man, who has
such a gift for languages, has so little dramatic perspicacity that he cannot distinguish
in this dialect many words foreign to the
Spanish. He pretends that only the roots
of Sanscrit words have been preserved. I

like the odor of the perfume which you have
sent me; I like it less, however, since I have
learned that the one who gave it to you sees
you often.

CCLXXXIX.

PALACE OF SAINT-CLOUD,
August 20, 1866.

DEAR friend, I received your letter yesterday.   I thank you for your compliments
on my appointment as a grand officer of the
Legion of Honor.   It surprised me as much
as you.   I say to myself, like the " Cocu
Imaginaire ":

" Does one's leg become more crooked,
after all, or one's shape less graceful ? "

I beg your pardon for quoting a play
which you have not read because of its
title.

You take a singular route to go to the
land of the sea lions; but if you can have a
little sunlight, you shall have a great deal of
pleasure in seeing the banks of the Loire.
There is nothing more French in France.   I
recommend to you the palace of Blois,
which was recently restored.   Inspect the

new church of Tours, restored.   It is situated on the Rue Royale, at the right from the station.   I forget the name of it.   See also, at Tours, a house which is called, improperly, the house of the executioner, and which is attributed to Tristan l'Ermite, because of a sculptured cord girdle at the windows, attribute of a widow, which the ignorant have taken for a hangman's rope.

We have deplorable weather.   Yesterday I had a long drive.   We were caught in a storm, which wet me to the bones.   The water filled the cushions, so that we were as in a bath-tub.   I shall be in Paris, I think, in the last days of this month, and will go to Biarritz in the beginning of September. Will you come ?

The Emperor is in good health.   We pass the time without etiquette.   We dine in frock coats, and everybody does as he pleases.   I have received from Russia an enormous history of Peter the Great, written from a quantity of official documents, hitherto unpublished.   It seems to me that everything tends to peace.   It is very evident that M. de Bismarck is a great man,

and too well prepared for anybody to be
angry against him.   We shall have to digest
a great many things until we get the needle
gun.   What the German parliament will do
remains to be seen.   As for Italy, it is not
even mentioned.   Good-by, dear friend.

CCXC.

BIARRITZ, *September 24th.*

WE have four days of rain in seven.   The
three others are hot.   The sea is much more
beautiful here than at Boulogne.   I went to
an amusing excursion in the mountains, the
other day, and saw one of the strangest
grottoes that one may see.   You pass under
a great natural bridge, made of one arch, as
long as the Pont Royal; you have, on one
side, a wall of rocks, and, on the other side,
a tunnel, natural also, and very long; for
nature, less clever than engineers, made its
bridge lengthwise and extended it with the
tunnel.   Under the tunnel, perpendicular to
the bridge, runs a clear brook.   The propor-
tions are gigantic.   It is very cool there and
at a thousand leagues from human beings.

This beautiful place, which is called simply Sagarramedo, is in Spain; and if it were near Paris, an enterprising man would show it for ten cents and make his fortune. In another cavern, at a league from there, but in France, we found a score of smugglers, who sang Basque songs in chorus, with the accompaniment of the " galoubet." It is a little, shrill flute, very savage and very agreeable. The music is full of character, but sad enough to bury the devil, as are all the tunes of mountaineers. We were guided there by a singular man, who has made a fortune by smuggling. He is the king of these mountains, and everybody obeys him. Nothing could have been more beautiful than to see him gallop among the rocks on our column's flank, which had a great deal of trouble to go through the pass. He leaped over all obstacles, yelling to his men in Basque, in French, and in Spanish, and never making a false step. The Empress had charged him with watching over the Prince Imperial, whom he made pass with his pony through the most impossible routes which you may imagine, and with as much care of him as if he had been a lot of prohibited goods. We stopped for an hour at his house at San, where we were received by his daughters, who are well-bred persons, well dressed, and not at all provincial, different from Parisians only by the way in which they pronounce " r," which, for the Basques, is always " rrrh."

We expect the fleet; but the sea is so bad that, if it came, we could not communicate with it. There is no crowd at Biarritz. There are few pretty faces. Nothing can be uglier than the women's bathing dress. I have been presented to the Grand Duke Luchtenberg. I have discovered that he reads Schopenhauer, believes in positive philosophy, and is inclined to socialism. I expect to be in Paris in the first days of October. Will you be there? Good-by, dear friend.

CCXCI.

Paris, *November* 5, 1866.

WE shall be, therefore, like Castor and Pollux, who never could appear on the same horizon! Besides the pleasure which I would have had in seeing you, I expected that of reading to you something which I have translated from the Russian. At Biarritz, they were disputing one day on the difficult situations in which a person might be; as, for example, Roderigue between his papa and Chimène, Mademoiselle Camille between her brother and the Curiace. At night, having drank tea which was too strong, I wrote a score of pages on such a situation. The thing is very moral, at bottom, but there are details to which Monseigneur Dupanloup might object. There is also a begging of the question, necessary for the development of the tale. Two persons of different sex go to an inn. This has never happened, but it was necessary for my tale, and near them something extraordinary happens. It is not, I think, the worst thing that I have written, although it is written in haste. I read it to the lady of the house. There was at Biarritz, the Grand Duchess Marie, daughter of Nicholas, to whom I had been presented several years ago. We renewed our acquaintance. Soon

after my lecture I received the visit of a
policeman, saying that he had been sent by
the Grand Duchess. "What may I do for
you?"—"I have come from her Imperial
Highness to ask you to come to her to-night
with your novel."—"What novel?"—
"The one which you read, the other day,
to her Majesty." I said that I had the
honor of being her Majesty's jester, and
could not work for others without her permission. I ran at once to relate the thing
to her. I expected that the result would be
a war with Russia, and it mortified me a
little to be not only permitted to go, but
asked to accompany the policeman to the
Grand Duchess's. In order to console myself, I wrote a letter to the Grand Duchess,
announcing my visit. I went to carry my
letter to her house; there was a great deal
of wind, and, in a far-off alley, I met a woman whom her skirts, into which the wind
had entered, threatened to blow into the
sea. She was in the greatest embarrass-
ment, blinded and dazzled by the noise of
her crinoline and the rest. I ran to her aid.
I had a great deal of trouble in aiding her,

18

and then only I recognized the Grand
Duchess. She acted very well with me; she
gave me good tea and some cigarettes, for
she smokes, as all Russian ladies do. Her
son, the Duke of Luchtenberg, is a very
handsome fellow. Good-by, dear friend.
What do you think of overflows? I congratulate you on not having been drowned.

CCXCII.

CANNES, *January* 3, 1867.

DEAR friend, your letter filled me with remorse. I have wanted to write to you for a
long time, but the uncertainty as to where
you are is a great bother. You are ever
wandering, and none knows where to catch
you. Then, you have not replied to a very
long letter, written in a very beautiful style,
which I sent to you. Moreover, you do not
know how time flies in a land like this,
where it never rains, and where the most
important thing is to stay in the sun. I
have done nothing but read a history of
Peter the Great. The great man was a bar-
barian, who got drunk horribly. This did

not prevent him from being superior to his
time.   I should like to say that, some day,
to persons as prejudiced as you are.   I am
reading the novel of my friend, Madame de
Boigne.   It pains me.   She is a person of
much wit, who exposes her faults and criti-
cises them bitterly, but persists in them.
She passed more than thirty years without
saying a word of this novel, and she ordered
its publication in her will.   It surprised me
as much as if I heard that you printed a
treatise on geometry.

CCXCIII.

PARIS, *Thursday, April* 4, 1867.

DEAR friend, here I am, at last, in Paris.
I did not write to you, because I was too
sad and could say only painful things of
myself and of this sublunar world.   You will
find me very ill, but very happy to see you.
If the weather be fine Friday morning, we
may go together to the Museum of the
Louvre.   I hardly dare to go out, because I
fear the cold, but am ordered to take exer-
cise.   I hope you are still prosperous.   They

are repairing my house, and I am reduced to living in my parlor, which is as sad as a prison. Come to console me. You may take all the books you want and I will not ask you to leave anything in pawn. Good-by.

CCXCIV.

PARIS, *Friday, April* 30, 1867.

DEAR friend, I am very sorry that you are surrounded by sick persons. I fear that you are not thinking of me. Will you not come to take care of me ? I went to the exposition and was not dazzled. It is true that it was raining and impossible for me to see the amusing things which are in the garden. I saw some beautiful Chinese objects, too high priced for my purse, and Russian carpets, all sold. Some morning you shall have to take me there and guide me in my purchases. The rainy weather hurts me much. I do not dare to go out and I live like a bear. I am burning with the desire to go to your house some evening, but I am convinced that I should be compelled to spend the night on the first step of your stairway.

CCXCV.

Wednesday, June 26, 1867.

DEAR friend, would it not have been better if you had brought your bouquet to me yourself ? I have condoled with you for the loss of your purse at the exposition. Condole with me, for I have lost mine in a carriage.

CCXCVI.

PARIS, June 30, 1867.

DEAR friend, here are two tickets for to-morrow's ceremony. They deserve a big tip, for I had a great deal of trouble in obtaining them. I send them to you in haste. Try not to be ill. It will be terribly hot.

CCXCVII.

Friday, July 5, 1867.

DEAR friend, I am charmed that you enjoyed yourself. I was afraid of the heat. You sought for me vainly; I was not there. Come quickly to relate to me the beautiful things which you saw and to give me your opinion of the Sultan and of the princes, who had the great privilege of contemplating you for three hours.

CCXCVIII.

PARIS, *July* 27, 1867.

DEAR friend, I thank you for your letter. I shall not describe to you all my ills, but pray believe that I am overcome by them. I hope that you will pity me.   I do not sleep nor eat.   I envy you these two faculties, which you possess with many others.

I congratulate you on having met the Sultan.   Was he amiable ?   The opera people are discontented with him.   They like better Egypt's Pasha.   He has been reconciled with his cousin, Mustapha, but they would not drink coffee together, each one being persuaded that it would be too dangerous, because of the great progress of chemistry, I suppose.   If you had been in Paris, you would have seen something beautiful which was given to me.   It is a brooch in the form of a shield, with a portrait of Marie Antoi-

nette in miniature, made, probably, at
Vienna, before her marriage, and given by
her to the Princess de Lamballe. There
was a lock of her hair behind it, but somebody took it. I sent the brooch to her
Majesty, who is making a collection of objects of Marie Antoinette. It will be, certainly, one of its prettiest relics. It is au-
thentic, and was worn for a long time by
Princess de Lamballe. I hold these sad
antiquities in horror, but one should not
dispute about tastes.

I think you might have been a little more
polite, and borrowed my proofs from me.
Sainte-Beuve is still ill. There is a great
number of women around him. When are
you coming back ? I need you to tell me
stories and make me take my ills patiently.
I read Luther's Table Talk, the other night.
That big man pleases me, with all his prejudices and his hatred for the devil.

CCXCIX.

PARIS, *September* 6, 1867.

DEAR friend, I have received your letter,
which gave me much pleasure. I went, the

other day, to the exposition, where I saw
the Japanese women. They have a coffee-
and-milk complexion, which is very agrec-
able. As far as I could judge by the folds
of their gowns, they have legs as thin as
those of a chair, which is pitiful. While I
looked at them, I said to myself that Euro-
pean women would not appear so well before a Japanese public. Do you imagine
yourself exhibited at Yeddo, and Prince
Satsuma's grocer saying, " I would like to
know if the bump in the back of this lady's
gown belongs to her ? " Talking of bumps,
they are not wearing them at all, and this
proves that there were none; for all women
found themselves at the same instant in the
fashion.

CCC.

PARIS, September 27, 1867.

THERE is a Prince Augustin Galitzin, who
has become converted to Catholicism, and
who is not very clever in Russian. He has
translated a novel by Turgenieff, the title
of which is " Smoke." Turgenieff asked
me to correct the proofs. Well, there are
vivacious things in this novel which make

Prince Galitzin blush. For example, an un-
heard-of thing: a Russian princess in love,
with aggravation of adultery. He skips the
passages which wound him too much, and I
reëstablish them in the text. He is sometimes very sensitive, as you will see. The
princess comes to see her lover in a hotel,
at Baden. She goes into his room, and the
chapter finishes. The story resumes, in the
Russian original, as follows: "Two hours
later, Litvinof was alone on his divan."
The new Catholic has translated as follows:
"An hour later, Litvinof was in his room."
You see, it is much more moral, because
it suppresses an hour, and thus diminishes
the sin by half. Moreover, room, instead of
divan, is much more virtuous: a divan en-
tails guilty acts. I have reestablished the
two hours and the divan; but the chapters
wherein I have done this have not been pub-
lished. This amuses me very much. There
is a beautiful scene in the novel, wherein the
heroine tears English lace, which is much
more grave than a divan. I am waiting to
see what they will do when they reach this
passage.

CCCI.

PARIS, *Monday night, October* 28, 1867.

I AM still ill, hardly breathing, and on the eve of not breathing at all. The sudden death of M. Fould has grieved me much. I expect to go out of town in the first days of November. I am urged to go, in order to escape a cold. Good-by, dear friend; I hope you will return before my departure. Quit the ugly fog, and take good care of yourself.

CCCII.

PARIS, *November* 8, 1867.

DEAR friend, I write to you in haste. I shall go to Cannes to-morrow, to get sunlight and heat. I do not know how long I shall be able to remain out of town. It depends on the Pope, Garibaldi, and M. de Bismarck. The Pope is convinced that he owes no obligation to us, and that it was heaven which did everything for his beautiful eyes. Good-by, dear friend.

CCCIII.

CANNES, *December* 16, 1867.

FINE weather has returned and I am beginning to breathe again. I am at the mercy of every change of the weather, and there is not a barometer which I may not surpass by the sureness of my predictions. I am much frightened by politics; there is, in the general tone of the journals and of the orators, something which recalls 1848 to me. There are strange fits of anger, without apparent causes. All nerves are strained.

CCCIV.

CANNES, *January* 5, 1868.

DEAR friend, forgive my belated answer. I have been, and am still, ill. The cold hurts me a great deal. I am anxious for my good friend, Panizzi, who is ill in London. The last news which I had from him, shows that he is discouraged, which is a very bad symptom in patients. I am reading a book which is too long, and badly written, but the author of which is honest and says what he has seen and heard. One must not dwell on his reflections, for he is a little foolish. It is Dixon's " New America." He saw the Mormons and the republic of Mount Lebanon. This and Fenianism give an idea of America. Good-by, dear friend; I wish you good health and prosperity.

CCCV.

CANNES, *February* 10, 1868.

I HAVE not become accustomed to suffer and suffering irritates me. This gives me two ills, instead of one. I think I will stay here until the end of the month. I am glad that my essay on Pushkin pleased you. I wrote it without having the works of Pushkin by me. The verses which I quoted were those which I learned by heart, in the time of my Russian fervor. There never has been here as great a number of English men and women. The women have incredible hair, gowns, and red stockings. Among the extraordinary Englishmen is the Duke of

Buccleugh, who has a horn in the middle of his forehead. His son has an inclination to imitate him. Do not think that I say this metaphorically. It is a real horn growing in the cranium.

CCCVI.

MONTPELLIER, *April* 20, 1868.

DEAR friend, I have been so ill as to lose all courage. It was impossible for me to think. I learned, by chance, that there was at Montpellier a physician who treated asthma by a new method and I have tried it. It seems to me that my condition is improving. I hope to find you soon in Paris. There is a fair under my windows. They are exhibiting a giantess, in a satin gown, which she lifts to show her legs. Their diameter is that of your waist. Good-by, dear friend.

CCCVII.

PARIS, *June* 16, 1868.

I WENT, day before yesterday, to the Bois de Boulogne, where I saw the most extrava-

gant gowns.   I met a very beautiful woman,
whose hair was the color of an aurora.   I
could have sworn that she was a Breda
street girl.   I recognized in her the wife of
a general.   Her hair was formerly a dark
chestnut.   We are progressing in manners.

CCCVIII.

PALACE OF FONTAINEBLEAU,
August 4, 1868.

I HAVE been here for a fortnight, doing
nothing at all.   I have a sweet memory of
our last walk.   Have you ?   Here I walk a
little, read less, and breathe well enough.
There are about thirty persons in the palace, the only new comers being cousins of
the Empress, whom I met in Madrid, and
who are very amiable to me.   I have made a
copy of a portrait of Diane de Poitiers.   She
is represented as Diana, dressed with a bow
and arrow, and it is evident that she posed.
From the feet to the head, everything is a
portrait.   I shall dare to say that the fact
results, from an examination of her legs,
that she tied her garters above her knee.

This was the fashion of her time.   It is not the fashion now, I have heard.

CCCIX.

PARIS, *September 2,* 1868.

WHILE I was at Fontainebleau, a strange thing happened to me.   I had the idea of writing a novel for my hostess, and did not have the time to finish it.   I finished it here, but I had no sooner done this than I began another novel.   This recrudescence of the malady of my youth alarms me, because it resembles a second childhood.   When I was in the palace we read prodigious novels, whose authors were unknown to me.   It is to imitate them that I wrote this last novel. The scene is in Lithuania, where they talk pure Sanscrit.   A great lady of the land, having gone to hunt, has had the misfortune to be captured by a bear, destitute of sensitiveness.   She becomes insane, but gives birth to a boy, who grows and becomes charming, only he is inexplicably odd.   He gets married, and on the night of his wedding, eats his wife raw.   You, who divine

everything, because I tell you everything,
guess why.   That charming boy is the ille-
gitimate son of that badly bred bear. Please
tell me what you think of it.   Good-by,
dear friend; write to me more than three
words on a line. Tell me very candidly what
you think of the bear.

CCCX.

PARIS, *Tuesday, September 29, 1868.*

DEAR friend, the principal thing is that
the lecture did not tire you. Is it possible
that you did not guess at once how badly
bred that bear was ? As I read, I saw on
your face that you disapproved of the plot.
I shall have to submit to yours.   Do you
think that the reader, less timorous than
you, will accept your version ? So it is a
simple look of the bear which made that
poor woman insane and gave to her son his
sanguinary instincts.   It shall be done as
you wish.   Your advice to me has always
been good; but this time, I think, you
abuse the permission which you have to
criticise me adversely.   I shall go to Mont-

pellier Saturday. I hope to say good-by to you two or three times before then.

CCCXI.

CANNES, *November* 16, 1868.

I HAVE been for six weeks coughing and stifling, and the different drugs which I take, with much docility and resignation, produce no effect upon me. I sleep badly and spend the time entertaining blue devils. It is at night especially that I suffer.

I made, during my insomnia, a careful copy of the " Honey Hunter," with the changes that you advised and which seem to me to improve the work. That the bear went to the extreme of troubling an illustrious genealogy remains doubtful. Still, intelligent persons like you will understand that a very grave accident occurred. I have sent this new edition to M. Turgenieff, so that he may revise the local color. The trouble is that neither he nor I have been able to find a Lithuanian who knew his language and his country. I wished to send this work to the

19

Empress for her birthday; but I have resisted the temptation and have done well.
God only knows what would have become of
the bear in the society of Compiègne.

Poor Rossini is dead. It is said that he
worked a great deal although he wished to
publish nothing. This has always seemed
to me to be improbable. Consideration of
money had always a great importance for
him. He was one of the wittiest men I
have met, and there was nothing more marvellous than the air of the "Barber of
Seville" sung by him. No actor was com-
parable to him. If you know some amusing
book, tell me about it, I pray you.

CCCXII.

CANNES, *January* 2, 1869.

IF you knew what an ugly, what a monotonous life I am leading, you would understand that it is bad enough to endure it
without rendering an account of it. The sky
and the sea are magnificent, and their influence, which formerly gave me health, does

me no good now. What shall I do ? I do
not know, but I have often a great desire
that all would end. Your voyage seems to
be agreeable, but I do not approve of your
return through the Tyrol. You will meet
with a great deal of snow; you will lose the
skin of your cheeks. Any other road
would be better. Why do you not go to
Sicily and see Mt. Ætna, which is in erup-
tion, they say ? I have copied again " The
Bear," with much care. Many things in it
are changed, for the better, I think. Title
and names are changed also. For persons
as unintelligent as you, the manners of that
bear will remain very mysterious. But one
will not be able to argue from them to his
disadvantage, however perspicacious one
may be. An infinity of things remain un-
explained in the story. Physicians tell me
that plantigrades may, better than other
beasts, ally themselves with us; but such
cases are scarce, naturally, bears not being
very attractive. Good-by, dear friend, I
wish you a happy new year.

CCCXIII.

CANNES, *February* 23, 1869.

I FIND, dear friend, that my ill is incurable. I have tried I do not know how many infallible remedies; I have been in the hands of three or four very skilful men, not one of whom gave me the slightest relief. I have not the strength to read, and I have no books. I think that you will find my " Bear " better presentable in his new form. I have made illustrations for the book. Do not think that they include all the scenes, the one, for example, where the bear forgets himself. Good-by, dear friend; I regret that you are not going to Rome this year.

CCCXIV.

CANNES, *March* 19, 1869.

DEAR friend, I have been in peril for four or five days. I can walk in my room now, and may soon, I am told, go out in the sunlight. Good-by, dear friend. Health and prosperity.

CCCXV.

CANNES, *April* 23, 1869.

DEAR friend, I shall leave here day after to-morrow. I am very weak, but think I may endure travel. I hope to find you in good health. Good-by, dear friend.

CCCXVI.

PARIS, *Sunday, May* 2, 1869.

DEAR friend, I have been in Paris for several days, but I was so tired and so ill that I had not the courage to write you. Come to see me and console me. Good-by.

CCCXVII.

PARIS, *May* 4, 1869.

I AM sorry that you did not wait two minutes. You would not let the servant tell me that you had come and simply gave him my book. You call this a visit to a patient! Your charity was easy. It does not count. I am a little better and I need you to go to the exposition, where I do not wish to

see daubs and nudities. You shall be my
guide. Do you remember the time when I
was yours ? Good-by, dear friend.

CCCXVIII.

PARIS, *Saturday, June* 12, 1869.

DEAR friend, I am afflicted by the profound stupidity evident in public affairs.
This people, which believes itself to be the
wittiest on earth, expresses its desire to
enjoy a republican form of government by
demolishing the stands where poor people
sell newspapers. The danger is that there
is a sort of emulation for stupidity, as for
everything else.

I spend my time deciphering letters of
the Duke of Alba and of Philip II., which
the Empress gave to me. They wrote like
cats. I am beginning to read Philip II. easily,
but his captain-general still embarrasses me.
I have just read one of his letters to his august master, written a few days after the
death of Egmont, in which he pities the fate
of the countess who has not one loaf of
bread after having had a dowry of ten thou-

sand florins. Philip II. has a long and
troubled way of saying the simplest things.
It is very difficult to guess what he wants,
and it seems that his constant aim is to em-
barrass his reader and leave him to his own
devices. They made the most hateful pair of
men that ever existed, and, unfortunately,
neither was hanged, which is not flattering
to Providence. Good-by, dear friend.

CCCXIX.

PARIS, *June* 29, 1869.

I THANK you for your letter, dear friend.
I am angry against poets and pretended
temperate climates. There is no spring,
there is not even summer. I went out of
doors to-day and came back frozen. When
I think that there are people who go in the
woods and talk of love in weather so cruel,
I am tempted to believe in miracles.

I am going to Saint-Cloud Thursday,
where I shall remain probably a fortnight.
I am reading, with a great deal of trouble,
Renan's " Saint Paul." He has decidedly
a monomania for landscapes. Instead of

doing his work, he describes woods and prairies. I have received the works of Baudelaire, which have made me furious. Baudelaire was crazy! He died in the hospital, after writing verses which attracted for him the esteem of Victor Hugo, and which had no other merit than that of being immoral. Now they are making of him a misunderstood man of genius!

CCCXX.

PARIS, *Wednesday night, August* 5, 1869.

I SPENT a month at Saint-Cloud, in a tolerable condition. The open air did me good, I think. My physician of Cannes came with a new remedy, invented by him, which cured me of my painful oppression. It is an eucalyptus pill, and the eucalyptus is a tree of Australia, naturalized at Cannes. It is well, if it lasts, as the man said while he was falling from a fourth-story window.

At Saint-Cloud I read " The Bear " before a very select audience, among which were many young ladies, who did not understand, it seemed to me. This gives me the

idea to send the work to the " Revue,"
since it may cause no scandal. Tell me
what you think of the idea. You must keep
in mind the century's progress in hypocrisy.
Good-by, dear friend. Write me something
gay, for I am very sad. I have great need
of your gayety and of your real presence.

CCCXXI.

PARIS, *September* 7, 1869.

DEAR friend, I am beginning to look
toward the south, although I have not felt
yet the approach of winter, but I have promised myself not to be surprised by the cold.
I have taken baths of compressed air, which
have done me some good, and I am following a new treatment, which is successful
enough. I am still very solitary; I never
go out at night, and I see almost nobody.
At Saint-Cloud the Empress had made me
read "The Bear "—it is called " Lokis " now,
which means bear in Jmoude—before young
girls who, as I think I told you, understood
nothing at all. This encouraged me, and,
on the 15th of this month, the thing will

appear in " La Revue des Deux-Mondes."
The Emperor's illness is not grave, but it
may be prolonged.   I shall write this winter
a life of Cervantes to serve as a preface for
a new translation of Don Quixote.   Is it a
long time since you have read Don Quixote ?
Does it amuse you still ? Do you know
why ? It amuses me and I cannot tell the
reason; on the contrary, I know many reasons which should prove that the book is
bad; and yet it is excellent.   I should like
to know your ideas on this subject.   Do
me the pleasure of reading a few chapters
and of asking yourself questions about
them.   Good-by; I hope that the month
will not go by without my seeing you.

CCCXXII.

CANNES, *November* 11, 1869.

DEAR friend, I am here in the finest
weather imaginable, and the most persistent,
which makes the gardeners despair, for they
cannot make their cabbages grow.   I am not
better than if the weather were bad.   Then
I have had grave troubles.   The servant

whom I had brought with me became suddenly so impertinent that I had to discharge
her. You can understand how disagreeable it
is to lose a servant who has been with one for
forty years. Fortunately, repentance came.
She asked for forgiveness so persistently
that she gave me a pretext to yield and keep
her. She has so many good qualities that
it would have been impossible for me to replace her. I hope that my firmness shall
have a salutary effect in the future and prevent similar incidents.

CCCXXIII.

CANNES, *January* 6, 1870.

DEAR friend, I thank you for your letter
and for your good wishes. I did not have
the material force to reply at once. The
cold has hurt me much. I am discouraged;
nothing does me good. I try all the remedies and they have no effect. I have the
certainty that a slow and painful death is
coming to me. I must make the most of it.

Politics do not give me an agreeable diversion. It seems to me that we are march-

instant that I would commit the indiscretion of dying at the house of a person whom I did not know intimately enough to take that liberty. I came here in very bad condition. I was better yesterday. I hope to go to Paris at the end of the month. I ask myself often if I could go up my stairs. You know so many things, do you know an apartment where I could be installed without having to go up many steps ? Good-by, dear friend; take good care of yourself. Health is the best of this world's goods.

CCCXXVI.

CANNES, *May* 15, 1870.
I AM horribly weak; yet have the hope to go to Paris at the end of next week. My health is absolutely ruined. I wish I could find diversion in work, but work requires a strength which I have not.

CCCXXVII.

PARIS, *June* 26, 1870.
DEAR friend, I have been ill for a month. I can do nothing, not even read. I suffer a

great deal and have little hope. I have put
some order in the shelves of my library,
and keep for you the " Lettres de Madame
de Sévigné," in twelve volumes, and a small
Shakespeare. When you come to Paris, I
will send them to you. I thank you for
thinking of me.

CCCXXVIII.

PARIS, *July* 18, 1870.

DEAR friend, I have been, and am still,
very ill. I think that one must be in very
good health and have very strong nerves
not to be affected by the events of to-day.
I do not need to tell you what I feel about
the war with Prussia. I am one of those
who think that it could not be avoided. The
explosion might have been retarded, but it
was impossible to avert it. War is more
popular here than it ever was. Military men
are full of confidence, but when one thinks
that all the future is subject to the chance
of a bullet, it is difficult to share that confidence. Good-by, dear friend. The physi-

cians say that I am better, but I do not feel
so.   Good-by; I kiss you with all my heart.

CCCXXIX.

PARIS, *Tuesday, August* 9, 1870.

DEAR friend, I think that you would do
well not to come to Paris.   There are in
the streets only discouraged people, or
drunken men singing the Marseillaise.   The
army has been admirable, but it seems that
we have no generals.   I am not worse, only
overwhelmed by the situation.   I am writing to you from the Luxembourg, where we
do nothing but exchange hopes and fears.
Good-by.

CCCXXX.

PARIS, *August* 29, 1870.

DEAR friend, I thank you for your letter.
I am very ill and very nervous.   Affairs
have improved a little.   The military men
show confidence.   It seems that Marshal
Bazaine's army achieved prodigies of valor.
The Prussians are conducting the war by

force of numbers. Until now they have
been successful, but near Metz the carnage
was such as to cause sad reflections to them.
It is said that the young ladies of Berlin
have lost all their dancers. If we can lead
the rest to the frontier, or bury them here,
which would be better, our troubles will not
yet be at an end. This terrible butchery is
only the prologue to a tragedy, the last
scene of which no one knows. Whether we
are victorious or defeated, a revolution must
come. All the blood that has been shed
is to the profit of the Republic—that is, of
organized disorder. Good-by, dear friend;
remain where you are. Here, we are very
quiet; we are waiting for the Prussians with
a great deal of calmness.

CCCXXXI.

CANNES, *September* 23, 1870.

DEAR friend, I am very ill, so ill, that to
write is very difficult. There is some im-
provement. I will write to you soon, I
hope, in detail. Send to my house at Paris

for the " Lettres de Madame de Sévigné "
and the Shakespeare. I should have sent
them to you, but I went away.   Good-by;
I kiss you.

Prosper Mérimée died two hours after
writing this letter.

Printed in the United Kingdom
by Lightning Source UK Ltd.
121842UK00001B/17/A